God's Desire is *You*

*A revelation
of the
prophetic
words of love found in
the Song of Solomon*

*I am my Beloved's and
His desire is for me.*

Song of Solomon 7:10

This book is dedicated to my husband Jim. His love for me has been a reflection of God's supernatural love for all of us. However, learning to love as I should has come with a wonderful, challenging, training process in both relationships. As the Holy Spirit gently wooed me to the reality of becoming the bride of Jesus, my spiritual Husband, I was also set free to be a loving wife to my physical husband. The lessons evolved into the stories in this book.

Table of Contents

Prayer

Lord, I ask You to please speak to me through the words of this book as I read. Open my heart to hear Your words of love for me. Expand my ability to understand and receive your passionate love and the destiny that is mine as I live in the revelation of Your glory. Amen

Introduction

Song of Solomon is a poetic prophecy that describes mankind's relationship to God, whose name is also Love. *God is Love.* (I John 4:16) To crave love is in our DNA. *We love because He first loved us.* (I John 4:19) Right now, the Holy Spirit is in a divine pursuit of romance with His bride (us) as He woos and draws us to Himself.

God's Desire is You illuminates the soul's journey into the Spirit realm as the Bride of Christ.

Key words found in the story are meant to move us past the logic of our natural thinking. Only our spirit-man can discern the treasures found in this book. *For the natural man does not receive the things of the Spirit of God; for they are foolishness to him, and he cannot understand them, because they are spiritually appraised.* (I Corinthians 2:14)

Many people are having dreams and visions from God's Holy Spirit. They are given to help us unlock the secrets found in the scriptures, and to reveal personal insight into His plans for our lives.

Jesus said, *My sheep hear my voice and they follow me.* (John 10:27) Heaven is speaking, and we have the privilege to hear. As we learn to know His voice our trust grows, and then by faith our adventure into His destiny begins.

God is the same today as in the past. He still desires to walk with us as He did with Adam. (Genesis 3:8) He wants face to face conversations with us just as he spoke with Moses. (Exodus 33:11) His plan has always been to share His majestic revelations with us as He did with John, and give us His wisdom to understand dreams as He did with Daniel and Joseph.

Each section of this book ends with a place to write the personal revelation you receive from the Spirit as you read. If you don't hear anything, just sit quietly for a few moments. Trust the truth that His sheep knows His voice. (John 10:27) Write down whatever comes to mind. Soon, surprising words of God's love and acceptance for you will fill the pages.

Enjoy the blessings that follow as you are stretched in exciting ways when heaven opens, and you enter into the fullness of His affection.

The Awakening

The Song of Songs was written by King Solomon. Let Him kiss me with the kisses of His mouth! For Your love is better than wine. (1-2)

In the verses of Solomon's song, he prophetically described God's plans for His bride. A maiden's spirit awakened to God's touch. This could have happened while in prayer or worship. Perhaps a mysterious dream stirred deep within her spirit. Or, even more baffling, she grasped supernatural insight from a whisper in the wind, or from the beauty of a mesmerizing white fluffy cloud. Possibly her heart was struck as life-giving words were spoken. Or, could it be, she saw one of the *Shining Ones* glowing brightly with God's glory and she thought *I want that*. Somehow, as only He can, the Holy Spirit awakened her spirit, and she longs for more of God's presence.

Touched by God's goodness, the maiden bravely asked for the intimacy of a kiss from her Lover who resides in another realm. She has no understanding of such an elusive thing, but she's willing to move past what she knows to receive a relationship beyond anything ever imagined. Is this possible?

In reality, it is the Holy Spirit who awakened her spirit. God created us with a spirit, soul, and body. The soul encompasses our minds, our will, and our emotions. God's divine plan is for our soul and flesh to bow to the leadership of our spirit-man, so we can live in unity with the Holy Spirit.

Passion to know God more fully stirred in the maiden. She realized true satisfaction isn't found in the things of the world. *The lust of the flesh, the lust of the eyes, and the pride of life* (I John 2:16) are losing their hold on her. She has an unexplainable yearning to know more about belonging to Jesus and His Kingdom.

Scriptures: *Awake, sleeper, and arise from the dead, and Christ will shine on you ...* (Ephesians 5:14)

Now may the God of peace Himself sanctify you entirely; and may your spirit and soul and body be preserved complete, without blame at the coming of our Lord Jesus Christ. (I Thessalonians 5:23)

Prayer: Father, Thank You for providing Jesus's perfect sacrifice for my life. I'm willing to learn what You have planned for my awakened spirit. Is it possible to be kissed by Jesus? I, too, yearn for something not quite explainable. I welcome You to awaken Your love in me, and reveal Your prefect will for my life.

His Fragrance

Your oils have a pleasing fragrance; Your name is like purified oil. **(1:3)**

Wanting to experience more of the realm of God's glory, the maiden spent time seeking to know Jesus better. She breathed deep with satisfaction as she imagined He was near. Suddenly, she realized the Holy Spirit's presence (oil) filled the air with a lovely, unknown, intoxicating fragrance.

This can also be our experience. Jesus desires communion with His bride. When we make the effort to get away from life's distraction to be with Him, He sometimes reveals Himself. He presses through the veil between earth and heaven, the physical realm and the spirit realm. As He comes near, the room fills with fragrance, and an awakened spirit can get a whiff of the essence of God.

People who've experienced the phenomena of His sweet aroma may describe what they smell differently, even though they're in the same place.

My first encounter with God's supernatural perfume was on a cold winter day when I'd gone to pray in a room with no windows. While thanking the

Lord for His goodness, the Holy Spirit interrupted, "I want you to be totally quiet for one hour."

Hmm. I'd come to pray. Quiet? No worship in my mind? Hmm. I don't think my mind's ever been quiet.

I bite my lips and wrestled with thoughts in an effort to find silence. Suddenly, after what felt like forever, a burst of fresh spring air filled the room as if windows were wide open with a breeze blowing. I breathed deep, just as I always do in the air of spring's delightful bouquet. Feeling the Holy Spirit moving around me, I knew this was a whiff of my Savior's presence. He had called me to the quiet time alone with Him, and He honored my efforts with the beauty of my favorite scent. No cologne could ever be created to copy the divine fragrance.

Therefore, the virgins love You. (1:3)

The virgins are other characters in this story. They also love and belong to the King. The maiden represents a leader, or forerunner, in God's Kingdom. As she leads, the whole body of Christ moves forward, because we're all connected in our spirits as one with Christ. She will lead the virgins on a path going higher, yet deeper into the fullness of the Kingdom of God.

Draw me after You and let us run together. (1:4)

As our spirit communes with the Holy Spirit, we begin to see with spirit-eyes and hear with spirit-ears. This is totally unnatural to human nature.

Prophetically, the maiden declared in this verse, "I'm ready to give up my will for Yours, but I don't know how. Lead me so we can live as One."

The Holy Spirit's desire is to be allowed to direct our lives. Giving up personal control is the price required for the privilege of knowing the secrets of God's supernatural kingdom. As we choose to follow Him, a battle arises between our spirit and flesh, and it can be quite a war. We're required to slow down, get quiet, and give up our own pursuits. But how else can we learn to hear the still small voice of God? By making this choice, we can come to know what David meant when he said *my soul follows hard after You* ... (Psalm 63:8)

Scriptures: ... *to you it has been granted to know the mysteries of the Kingdom of heaven* ... (Matthew 13:11)

Prayer: Holy Spirit, I give up control and yield my life to Your direction. This is hard to pray but I'm ready to give You my will. That's all I know to do right now. And Lord, if it's true we can smell Your

7

fragrance, I ask to know the beautiful scent of my God's presence.

My Revelation:

The King's Chambers

The King has brought me into His chambers.
(1:4)

Finding the time to get acquainted with God is challenging, but, oh, so wonderfully worth the effort. He has provided the human manual, His Word, to help us learn to know His character. The Bible also reveals who we are to Him. We are the focus of all His love.

The awakened maiden gave the Holy Spirit control of her life. By surrender, she supernaturally entered the Chambers of the King, one of many experiences He'll share with her in the Spirit realm.

...eyes have not seen, nor ear heard, or have entered into the heart of man the things God has prepared for those who love Him. (I Corinthians 2:9)

Chambers represent the rooms of our soul where the Holy Spirit lives. He often uses dreams to teach and awaken us to His world.

As I was seeking to know Him more deeply I had continual dreams of an old, dusty castle with a spiral staircase going up the center. The stairs had scaffolding all around as if it were under construction.

Rooms were being remodeled, and the Holy Spirit was the decorator. He enjoyed pulling things out of the closets and drawers and putting them on display as if they were too lovely to keep hidden. When a room was finished, I'd dream of being allowed to enter. His touch turned simple things I considered useless, unneeded, or forgotten into precious treasures.

The staircase was always unfinished in those dreams, so I wasn't allowed to climb them.

For a time, I was exhausted from all the remodeling going on while trying to sleep.

The Kingdom of God is within you. (Luke 17:21)

Houses in dreams represent the soul. The castle was me. I was under construction. His plan was to transform me into His home. I had no idea what completion would look like.

In one dream about my soul house, I was in the large garden. The fragrance of lovely flowers joined the breeze of the evening. A large fountain stood in the middle of a courtyard with water bubbling and flowing over each tier. A young man around thirty years old walked with me. The perfect romantic setting made me feel peaceful and content.

My companion began to speak of His affection for me. Even in my sleep, His expressions of love felt real and wonderful. His Words covered me with acceptance and admiration that brought joy. I felt whole.

His loving eloquence continued until I began to feel uncomfortable. He was moving too close, getting in my space. Pressing me with a passion I didn't know.

I lost my peace and contentment. After all, I didn't know this guy. What was He pulling? Just as if I put my arms out and pushed Him away, I backed off.

"You can't love me, I'm getting gray hair."

He pressed forward. "I love you."

I was unnerved by the attention. "You can't love me, I'm married."

Again, His eyes looked deep within me. "I love you."

In fear and frustration I said, "You can't love me, I'm old enough to be your Mother."

He didn't waver from any of my reasons for disqualification. "I love you."

I woke feeling the need to repent for dreaming about another man, but quickly Jesus whispered as if in secret, "It was Me."

"Oh, and what was the awesome feeling I had as You told me You loved me?"

"That was My unconditional love."

"Unconditional love is wonderful. It's what I've looked for all of my life. What I've longed for from my husband."

"That's what he's been longing for from you."

Ouch. That hurt. But it was true. I hadn't known such love was a possibility so how could I love him unconditionally?

Next morning, I shared the dream with Jim. He responded, "You sound like you've taken a lover."

My reply was, "Yes, I have. And by loving Him, I'll be able to love you the way I should."

That day I began my divine love affair with God. I was fearful, but I wanted it. I wanted Him. I couldn't push Jesus away or lose the feelings of His unconditional love because of my own inhibitions, fears, or stupidity any longer. I also needed to lay down my insecurities and quit pushing others away when they tried to get close.

Later, the Lord gave me even more depth of understanding about His love.

"Marian, I love everyone. I don't judge. No one is bad enough for Me to quit loving them. Think of the worse sinner you can."

Instantly, I thought of a person who would molest a child. To me, that was an unforgivable sin worthy of death. Children should be free to keep their innocence.

Knowing my thoughts, He responded. "I stand right beside all those in bondage to sin, waiting for them to quit pushing Me away because of their feelings of unworthiness."

Those words whirled through my head like a tornado, throwing everything I thought I knew about right and wrong, and good and bad, into the air spinning around. How could such a thing be true? As I contemplated the revelation, I knew it was time to have my mind reprogrammed by love. If this was how Love thought, I had a lot to learn.

Jesus paid the price for the worst possible sin. He desires to free people so they can receive His love. This reality convicted me. I knew I must look past the sin in people's lives and destroy judgment in my heart.

Quietly contemplating, I saw a vision of Jesus, filled with love, standing beside all people, longing to be allowed to help them live free. Then I knew, as His child, I am the one to show His unconditional love to others and help them meet their Savior. I yielded to being willing to be changed.

Scriptures: *Because he loves Me, I will deliver him, I will set him securely on high, because he has known My name. He will call on Me, and I will answer him. I will be with him and rescue him, and honor him with a long life. I will satisfy him and let him behold My salvation.* (Psalm 91:14-16)

... Mercy triumphs over judgment. (James 2:13)

Prayer: Lord, I ask for Your love to fill my mind. Help me look past the sin in other's lives so I can freely share Your love with them. May Your mercy living in me destroy the thoughts of judgment in my heart. Help me grasp the reality of Jesus standing beside everyone, loving them unconditionally. Display Your love through my life so they will be able to meet their Savior. Kill insecurity in me. Make me confident in You. I give You my fear so Your faith can be birthed in me. Replace my stupidity with divine wisdom. And Lord, I ask for dreams of my spirit house with the discernment to understanding what You reveal.

My Revelation:

Dark Soul

I am dark, but lovely, O daughters of Jerusalem, like the tents of Kedar. Like the curtains of Solomon. Do not look upon me because I am dark, because the sun has tanned me. My mother's sons were angry with me; they made me the keeper of the vineyards, but my own vineyard I have not kept. (1:5-6)

The maiden asked for a kiss from her Beloved. In reality, He already gave her love's first kiss on the cheek. God supernaturally awakened her spirit from a long sleep just as the prince did in *Sleeping Beauty*.

However, this was also a kiss of pure holiness. Each time Jesus reaches through the veil between heaven and earth and comes close, His holiness brings an awareness of our human impurity. His touch caused the maiden to seek for more, but she knew it was impossible to be good enough to belong to a holy King. In her mind she was unattractive and dark from laboring in the sun. Her family burdened her with their cares (vineyards prophetically are people), leaving no time for her to attend to her own life (her vineyard). Just like all humanity, she made excuses for her sinfulness.

15

By the King's divine presence, a seed of humility was planted in her heart. In His wisdom He showed her she was created to be His bride. She thought she fell far short of such a privilege because the same lies and deception covered her as is over most of humanity.

Everyone has a story as to why they don't measure up to the beauty God sees in them. Life brings rejections, broken hearts, and disappointments. Difficulties cause wounds and scars.

As we begin to experience the glory of God's Spirit realm, the truth of His love becomes evident, but for now, the maiden only knows herself to be dark (sinful), and Him to be light (pure).

But God looks at her through Jesus's perfect blood sacrifice. He never nags her about failures or shortcomings. Instead, He declares the truth of His finished work. She is beautiful, worthy, and delightful.

One day while in prayer, the Holy Spirit was ready to show me the condition of my soul. A vision revealed my inner-man to be black, dead, and void of any real life.

I was shocked. After all, I'd worked hard at being a faithful Christian for a long time. How could my soul be so horribly empty?

The Holy Spirit answered my thoughts. I was still the one in charge of my life, in my thinking (mind), desires and actions (will), and in all the ways I allowed myself to feel (emotions). Seeing the *truth* of who I was brought the same hopelessness the maiden described in these verses. What could I ever do to change?

Finally I understood the Holy Spirit wanted permission to move into my soul. He was the only One who could bring light and life into such darkness. That day, I yielded all of myself to God, but I questioned what He could possible do with someone so very dark.

The maiden felt the touch of holiness. She too, was aware of the hopelessness of her soul. But she also knew God saw her differently. A vision revealed she was to be the King's pure, holy bride.

Scripture: *... I came that they might have life, and might have it abundantly.* (John 10:10)

... God is light and in Him is no darkness at all. (I John 1:5)

The one who says he is in the light and yet hates his brother is in darkness ... (I John 2:9)

He delivered us from darkness and translated us into the Kingdom of His beloved Son. (Colossians 1:13)

You are a chosen race, a royal priesthood, a holy nation, a people for God's possession, that you may proclaim the excellences of Him who has called you out of darkness into His marvelous light. (I Peter 2:9)

Jesus said, I am the light of the world. He who follows Me shall not walk in the darkness, but shall have the light of life. (John 8:12)

Prayer: Lord, I repent of making excuses for my lack of holiness. Help me stop justifying my sinful actions. With fear and trembling, I ask Your holy presence to shine on the darkness of my soul and flood me with Your transforming light and life. Also, could I have a vision of who You see me to be? Thank You, Lord.

My Revelation:

Disciples

Tell me, O You whom my soul loves, where do You feed Your flock, where do You make it rest at noon. For why should I be as one who veils herself by the flocks of Your companions? (1:7)

The maiden's soul was refreshed as Love's freedom filled the dark emptiness she once knew. In youthful pestering or begging she asks for more. "Lord, it's You I want, and no other. Tell me how to find You? Where can I meet You, and eat with You? Please, please, please tell me." Then she added, "Well, at least let me know where to find others who have knowledge of You?"

The maiden repented, and gave God ownership of her mind, will, and emotions (soul). As He lovingly revealed her lifelessness she became aware of her need for fresh revelation in knowing His will and ways.

When our spirit-eyes open, we realize there is only a veil between earth and heaven, the natural and supernatural world. Heaven isn't far away. By faith, it is possible for us to step into the invisible realm of God's Kingdom. God can even manifest His presence and reveal Himself in our natural world.

This passionate maiden doesn't want any separation (veil) between them.

If you do not know, O fairest among women, follow in the footsteps of the flock, and feed your little goats beside the shepherd's tents. (1:8)

Paul set the example of a shepherd/leader when he said *Follow me as I follow Christ* (I Corinthians 11:1). Shepherds are those who care for God's people (flock). Tent is the place where believers gather. Goats represent the ones we are meant to disciple[2] as we teach them about the Kingdom life.

God is so good. He responded to her question with His positive love language. Instead of agreeing with her saying she was dark, He described her as fairest among women, and told her to, "Follow My people. They will provide what you need."

We need each other. Without a flock we can become dysfunctional, wandering sheep. Even though we don't enjoy the friction that comes with some relationships, we're kept fine-tuned by other people in our lives. *Iron sharpens iron, so one man sharpens another.* (Proverbs 27:17)

I liken you, my darling, to a mare harnessed to one of the chariots of Pharaoh. Your cheeks are beautiful with ornaments, (1:9-10)

The Bridegroom gave the maiden His instructions. He lavished her with praise to remind her who He saw her to be. Being encouraged, she wanted to do what He asks.

We too can accomplish far more with praise than criticism will ever achieve. Encouragement brings life and wholeness. Faultfinding and judgment will cause emotional death and destruction. This is a holy key with supernatural benefits in all relationships.

The Beloved watched the maiden's sincerity as she continually entrusted her heart to Him. And so, in the same way human love grows, their divine romance has progressed quickly. He needed to tell her of her advancement into purity because humility had come into her life. This virtue rarely sees its own progress.

Pharaoh's horses were the finest, most obedient, well-trained horses on earth. They were as disciplined as trained guards at a palace. When the horses stood waiting for the King, they wouldn't move. They didn't lift a foot or turn their heads. Discipline had trained them to stand as still as a statue.

In this verse, the Beloved is describing discipline and obedience. The maiden will learn these virtues as perfectly as Pharaoh's horses.

Earlier she asked that they might run together. (1:4) Her Beloved responded by telling her she is running like a champion horse. Secretly, the Holy Spirit carries her as fast as she is willing to move.

God is preparing her for the work of His end-time harvest. As the maiden yielded to her Beloved's voice, she realized she needed to lighten her load to move quickly when He called.

Cheeks prophetically represent the soul.[3] Ornaments describe things the Holy Spirit used to decorate her inner rooms. These aren't items such as lamps and pictures. The Spirit of God established the fruit of His character within her. He is love, joy, peace, patience, kindness, goodness, faithfulness, gentleness, and self-control. (Galatians 5:22) He is light (Ephesians 5:9) and righteousness (Philippians 1:11).

The décor designed by God's virtues now manifest in her sparkling eyes, and through the radiance of her joy-filled smile. The Designer's talent is evident in her pleasant voice tones as she shares encouraging words.

Her passion for possessions changed. Now she delights in life's simple pleasures. A calm spirit replaced stress and frustration. She freely praises God in the middle of a hectic day. God's virtues are evident when she relaxes in the pleasure of peaceful sleep. These are the ornaments of her life which decorate her with Kingdom beauty.

Your neck with strings of jewels (1:9-10)

An unyielded neck is stubborn (stiff-necked). The yielded maiden pleased her Beloved, so He gave her a necklace of precious stones and pearls. The Word, a pearl of great price (Matthew 13:46) has been hidden in her heart.

She has listened to her Father's instruction and they have become a chain to adorn her neck. (Proverbs. 1:9)

... Lips that speak knowledge are a rare jewel. (Proverbs 20:15)

We will make you ornaments of gold, studded with silver. (1:11)

How exciting. Here we see the Trinity (We) at work. They are busy getting ready for a wedding. The divine work of God's manifest presence (ornaments of gold), and Jesus's salvation (silver), created a crown for His Queen.

As she overcomes the challenges involved with learning obedience she will know the privilege of sitting with Jesus on His throne (Revelation 3:21), and wearing the Crown of Life the three Persons of the Trinity created for Jesus's bride.

Scripture: *Blessed are those who persevere under trial for once they have been approved, they will receive the crown of life, which the Lord has promised to those who love Him.* (James 1:12)

Prayer: Lord, today I ask You to take all thoughts causing depression or feelings of failure out of my mind. Help me hear Your words of love. Forgive me for being critical of others. Please show me how to connect with those who can help me mature in love. Teach me how to praise, honor, and encourage them. I'm beginning to understand the importance of Your discipline. Free me of the hindrances keeping me from winning people to you. Reflect Your character in me to reveal the purity of Your beauty and grace. Help me persevere in the preparations required to wear Your Crown of Life. I love You. Wow! I'm asking You to do things in me I didn't even know I would want a short time ago.

My Revelation:

The Table of the King

While the King was at His table (1:12)

While studying Song of Solomon, I realized entering into the fullness of God's supernatural Kingdom was being described as if there were different levels. Physically, the steps would be like climbing a mountain with the summit being Zion, the Holy habitation of God. (Joel 3:17)

As the story progresses, there are pauses where the maiden meets with the King. As they spend time together she's refreshed and prepared to continue her spiritual journey.

Going into unknown realms with God takes courage, trust, and supernatural faith. To find the fullness of the Spirit's plans at each level requires more dying to self.

And so, the maiden's climb took her to the level where the King is at His Table of Blessing. This place in the Kingdom reveals God's abundant goodness, provision, and answered prayers. It is only the beginning of many treasured places He has waiting for her.

The Table of Blessing is prepared to strengthen and encourage. Many Christians think they've arrived when they reach this place of God's many blessings. All their needs are provided, they are living in good health, and have enjoyable relationships. However, the handicap of this place is that it's hard to leave. Why would we want to? Life is so good.

While enjoying Jesus's blessings, the maiden must not settle down and stay in this place. She is to be flexible, ready to move when the Holy Spirit calls. Her joy will be even greater if she willingly pays the price required for her supernatural adventure.

She found the Lord's Table when she shut away to be alone with Him.[1] *Jesus said, I stand at the door and knock and if any man will hear my voice and open the door I will come in and eat with him and he with Me* (Revelations 3:20). Although this scripture is often referred to as God's call for us to open our hearts to salvation, it is also the Bridegroom asking His bride to open her life fully to Him. He knocks, wanting fellowship with His betrothed. When allowed to enter, He spreads a table, filled with heavenly things, before her.

While seeking to know the Lord more fully, my spirit-eyes and ears were opened to glimpses of God's Kingdom realm. I questioned if it was really possible to see His Table of Blessing. In answer, I saw, by the Spirit, a large wooden banquet table. The Holy Spirit asked me what I would like to have from His table.

In response, I questioned what He would choose to give me. For some time, when in prayer, the table would appear before me with one strange thing on it. Once it was a bowl of fruit. That was easy to understand. He wanted to give me the fruit of His Spirit. Then there was a pitcher of vibrant, luminous water. I heard *This is living water* (Holy Spirit) *to fill you to overflowing with abundant life.*

... Our lives will be as streams of water in a dry country ... (Isaiah 32:2)

Later, piles of ropes lay on the table. I asked what they were.

"The ropes are proof I've answered your prayers and set the people free who were bound by them."

I was thrilled to know God heard my prayers and responded.

Experiences with the Spirit come by taking time to be with Him, and learning to be quiet and listen. True communion with God is often spoken without human words. Perhaps, even without language, yet we understand. Reality starts when we believe by faith He is with us. He has promised to never leave or forsake us. (Hebrews 13:5)

The King is at His table waiting for fellowship with those He loves and longs to bless.

Scripture: *Behold a King will reign ... and the eyes of the blind will see and the ears of the deaf will listen and hearts will understand the truth.* (Isaiah 32:1-3)

I am with you always even to the end of the age. (Matthew 28:20)

Faith is the evidence of things unseen. (Hebrews 11:1)

You have prepared a table before me ... (Psalms 23:5)

Prayer: Lord, Thank You, for the possibilities of knowing You better. I ask You to open my spirit-eyes and ears to see the Spirit Realm. Help me know Your desire is to bless me with the experiences of the Table of Blessing. I choose to find time to wait quietly before You, and I open myself to receive the reality of Your Kingdom. Let my faith grow to see the unseen.

My Revelation:

Suffering

My perfume spreads its fragrance. A bundle of myrrh is my Beloved to me that lies all night between my breasts. **(1:13)**

The maiden came to know her God as *Good*. She spent time at His table enjoying the many blessings He lavished on her. In knowing Him, she found the freedom to become more like Him. Now, she has been allowed to smell her own fragrance, and recognized it's similar to the lovely essence of God.

This is the same as when my husband kisses me goodbye in the morning as he leaves for work. The aroma of his cologne lingers with me through the day because he pressed against me.

The perfume of God has overcome the maiden, and by their experiences together, humility destroyed pride. Faith dissolved fear. Truth overcame deception, and love is taking ownership of self. Her fragrance is a sweet smelling sacrifice to God.

From their times together, she knows her Beloved's scent as myrrh (suffering). No one wants to choose suffering, yet Jesus was a suffering Christ.[1]

We can only truly know Him to the extent we're willing to suffer for Him. She allowed pride, fear, deception, and even self to be destroyed until myrrh lies between her breasts. God's love has pressed these things from her life making all the past struggles worth it.

Remember the book of Job? Satan went to God's throne and asked permission to test him. The trials revealed Job's weakness, allowing him to belong even more fully to God. Job said, *The things I feared most have come upon me.* (Job 3:25) We too are tested to reveal our flaws. So, instead of fighting and getting frustrated when the tests come, wisdom would have us ask God where purity needs to be established. We're meant to learn our lessons quickly and completely, so there won't be any need for further testing in the same area. The word "test" has been described as *a tentative model for future experiment or development.*

God is so good He allows us to repeat exams if we fail. But it's painful to stubbornly refuse to learn, and then suffer with the same struggle over and over. Nothing makes me sadder than to watch those I love repeat another lap around the same mountain because they refuse to embrace God's best for them.

Rebellion and stubbornness will not enter the Kingdom of God. (Psalms 78:8)

We can find comfort in knowing the Holy Spirit allows some of the challenges we're meant to overcome. As His identity develops in us, we confirm we have what it takes to become royalty. Successfully passing the tests proves we're prepared to be the King's Bride.

In the Kingdom of God, it's considered advancement to realize we don't have it all together. So if it feels as if all hell has broken loose, don't despair. You've been allowed to enter into *His suffering*. Rejoice and don't give up. This is progress. Only His best friends share in His anguish. Paul proclaimed, ... *that I might know the fellowship of His sufferings* ... (Philippians 3:10)

In truth, Jesus has already paid the price for us by His perfect sacrifice, so we are only touched by the tests, not overcome.

Between my breast. (1:13)

When the word breasts is mentioned in Song of Solomon, we can know the word prophetically represent faith and love.[1] The maiden is aware those two virtues are developing more fully as Jesus lives in her heart. The experiences of the Refiner's fire with its frustrations and suffering are developing a heart of compassion for others. Her life will be purified as gold.

My Beloved is to me a cluster of henna blossoms from the vineyards of En Gedi. (1:14)

The maiden described her new fragrance as myrrh (suffering). By a whiff of her Beloved's presence she realizes He is as henna blossoms, meaning *ransomed price.* En Gedi was famous for the best fragrant flowers. He is as a divine heavenly garden.[1]

If we protect our flesh and cling to old habits we'll never know the scent described here. But by yielding and allowing our smelly flesh to die, it can become usable, just as fertilizer, for God's garden.

The bride-to-be sees lovely new things developing in her life (clusters). The blossoms create a sweet voice where once harsh words would have been spoken. The fragrance makes it possible for her to give preference to others instead of wanting her own way. Somehow, it keeps her from getting annoyed with the foolish choices other people make. Instead, she just loves them. To her surprise negative thoughts are disappearing. She's delighted with the life-giving encouragement she speaks without a thought. This new character, or personality, has been given to her like a surprise bouquet from heaven, and she feels rewarded.

Scripture: *For we are a fragrance of Christ to God among those who are being saved and among those who are perishing.* (I Corinthians 2:15)

Through many tribulations we must enter the Kingdom of God. (Acts 14:22)

... you have been distressed by various trials, that the proof of your faith, being more precious than gold which is perishable, even though tested by fire, may be found to result in praise and glory and honor at the revelation of Jesus Christ. (I Peter 1:6-7)

Beloved, do not be surprised at the fiery ordeal among you, which comes upon you for your testing, as though some strange thing where happening to you; but to the degree that you share the sufferings of Christ, keep on rejoicing; so that also at the revelation of His glory, you may rejoice with exultation. (I Peter 4:12-13)

Prayer: So this is what suffering is about. Show me where purity needs to be established in my life. I'm tired of all these tests. Lord, free me from stubbornness and rebellion. Those strongholds aren't working for me. Change my character to be kind and loving. Empower me with life-giving words to share with others. Oh, how I need Your help. I long to bear the fragrance of Your character.

My Revelation:

Beautiful

How beautiful you are, my darling! Oh, how beautiful! Your eyes are like doves. **(1:15)**

As I read my Bible, this verse really didn't have any meaning to me. Finally, God revealed He wanted me to receive His Words as my personal love letters from Him. I needed to choose to believe the truth of these sentences.

God Almighty wrote this for us. He thinks we're each uniquely beautiful. He calls us His darling, and He continually speaks the extraordinary words of this verse to us.

With a new mindset, I began to recognize the difference between what He says about me and the negative voices I heard in my head. My thoughts didn't align with His lovely words at all. This brought new determination to know I am who His Word describes me to be. Yielding to the Holy Spirit, I asked for the miracle of a transformed mind.

To my surprise, Jesus began to reveal Himself as a lavish lover. His words of passion were overwhelming, uninhibited God-sized expressions of affection. I had glimpses of my Beloved as all-encompassing.

The simplicity of His eloquent Words continually declares His longing for His bride. The words resonate through the heavens hoping everyone in the universe will hear.

As I learned to receive and accept His love language, it seemed the Holy Spirit in my heart was clapping His hands in joyful delight at the thought of me finally starting to know what He was always saying to me.

Meditating on this particular scripture, I paused on the word *Oh*. While quietly pondering this little word, it grew bigger and louder. The Creator of language found it so hard to express the beauty He was seeing in His bride, He had to stop, and then from the depths of the passion in His heart, our Ultimate God cried out in perfect expression.

"Oh."

The God of the entire universe is so overwhelmed with emotion for His bride He is reduced to a gasp. I love it!

Then for a second time, He said, "How beautiful." Can we still question His feelings for us when we know the powerful emotions expressed in these words? I think not. So, I declare, I will not doubt God's delight for me anymore. I am meant to own this verse as mine personally.

If God says we're beautiful, the truth is, we are beautiful. Jesus's blood has covered us with His finished work. Anything in our hearts which doesn't match the beauty He sees in us must go. Then our life will be free to align with who the Word says we really are.

I determined I wouldn't let my feelings of unworthiness push Him away any longer. His perfect sacrifice has already made me worthy. I chose instead to receive His love, and practice believing His Words about me were true.

As He gently, lovingly continued to share His abundant, ridiculous love for me, I began to relax and forget about my own opinion of myself. His love and acceptance brought with it new freedom.

Finally, I was able to pry unworthiness from my mind and lay it at His feet. I remember coming to Him with repentance for the ugly, hopeless things in my life. I felt as if I'd wrapped garbage in newspapers as the only gift I had to give my Beloved. To my surprise, He treated each package given as a great treasure.

And I loved the changes in me as I traded my worthlessness for His divine beauty. The transformation was so wonderful I started watching closely for anything else in my life that didn't reflecting His character so it could be exchanged for more of Him. Surrendering to His new life of love allowed Him to replace the useless things that thwarted my destiny. His constant love continually gave me more security to trust Him.

Your eyes are like doves.

Doves always represent the Holy Spirit and His purity. The King described the beauty of the maiden's eyes as a pure reflection of the Holy Spirit. *To the pure all things are pure ...* (Titus 1:15)

Scripture: *The Lord ... will beautify the meek with salvation.* (Psalm 149:4)

He makes all things beautiful in His time ... (Ecclesiastics 3:11)

Prayer: Jesus, I yield to Your love and truth. Help me believe this scripture is Your love letter to me personally. Set me free to know I am beautiful in Your eyes. I long to hear You say, "Oh" over my life. Open my spirit-ears so I hear clearly to receive this truth. By faith, I trade all my unworthiness and ugly garbage for Your love and beauty. Today, I choose not to doubt God is delighted with me. I, too, ask for the miracle of a transformed mind.

Our Verdant Bed

How handsome you are, my Lover! And so pleasant! Our bed is verdant. (1:16)

The human race often seems handicapped when it comes to sharing our feelings of love to others. Only when I began to hear the Exhorter personally did I learn how encouragement is meant to sound. In experiencing His passionate words, I hoped to be able to reveal my heart too.

The maiden heard pure words of approval from the One who loves her. Knowing *fear of rejection* has been destroyed, and newfound boldness has taken a seat, she feels ready to express her affection for Him. In her teenage manner she told her Mighty, Glorious Lover He is handsome and pleasant. Or, in other words, she likes Him.

In youthful expression she said, "Our bed is green," (verdant) meaning it's alive. Resting in this place of the Spirit is like laying in life. When we are *In Him*, He is the energizing life-source.

The bed mentioned in this verse agrees with the rest spoken of in Psalm 23:2. *He makes me lie down in green pastures; He leads me to waters of rest.*

As God, in His wooing ways, draws us to His supernatural, life-giving bed there is holy peace, quietness, and pure pleasure. The energizing restoration removes the heaviness carried through past struggles. Painful emotions are healed and the body is restored to health.

Come to me all you who are heavy laden and I will give you rest. (Matthew 11:28)

The beams of our house are cedars; our rafters are cypress. (1:17)

Through prophetic expression, we're given a glimpse of the place their courtship has taken the maiden. Imagine, as she relaxed on His bed of life, she looked up at the beautiful ceiling beams which are the support system of her spiritual palace. They are made of cedar with rafters of cypress. The red woods are used as a symbol of Jesus's perfect sacrifice as He shed His blood for us.[1]

This gives whole new understanding to the scripture… *I go to prepare a place for you.* (John 14:2) Our home is to be *In Him.* He is our protection just as supporting beams hold a roof up.

Scripture: *There remains therefore a Sabbath rest for the people of God. For the one who has entered His rest has himself also rested from his works, as God did from His. Let us therefore be diligent to enter that rest* ... (Hebrews. 4:9-11)

... He restores my soul ... (Psalm 23:3)

I will restore you to health and I will heal you of your wounds, declares the Lord ... (Jeremiah 30:17)

... I will make up to you for the years that the swarming locust have eaten ... (Joel 2:25)

Prayer: Lord, I choose to trade in the fear of rejection for a life of boldness. Please help me learn to be an exhorter. I ask for my voice and heart to be set free to share love extravagantly the way You do. Bring Your restoration into my life. Wipe out past pain and remove the heaviness that weighs me down. I long to know what it's like to lay in Your life-giving bed of energizing power.

My Revelations:

Holy Trade

I am the rose of Sharon, the Lily of the valleys.
(2:1)

Romance continues as lovers come to know each other. In the next few verses, we hear the words of their courtship. The maiden described herself as a wild rose. She thought she was as average as the lily of the valley that grew like weeds in the fields.[4]

I can relate. She has been shown there is destiny on her life, but she can't find anything special enough about herself to qualify her to belong to the King. But, that's okay. Self-approval isn't a Kingdom virtue anyway. If she thought herself worthy, she would be disqualified to fulfill God's divine purposes.

By eternal wisdom, the Spirit waits for her to give up trying to make herself good enough. Anyplace of self-approval, self-sufficiency, self-consciousness, self-serving, selfishness, or any self-word hinders the Kingdom life.

However, living in the Kingdom of God also creates a life in balance. We are meant to be free of self, yet understanding who we are *In Him*.

She will need to accept the fact she *can do all things through Christ who strengthens her,*

(Philippians 4:13) and she *is more than a conqueror through Him.* (Romans 8:37)

Finding the freedom of humility comes in knowing true power and love is ours only through Christ in us. So, we could question, was the maiden being humble describing herself as a wild rose, or were the words she spoke *self-condemnation*? That self-word looks similar to humility, but it is still a by-product of self, and is useable to the enemy to defeat us.

The difference is a person with false humility is fearful, weak, and powerless. Their mind is in despair, and they feel like a failure. Although self-condemnation seems to show pride has been destroyed, there could still be self in the heart. We don't want to leave any opening where the enemy can torment.

God never condemns us to teach us humility. Instead, He saturates us in love and holiness until we're melted in longing to surrender to Him. True humility brings strength and power through the Holy Spirit, which makes us bold.

While learning about holy humility, I read a book titled *Practicing the Presence of God,* which was about a monk named Brother Lawrence. He was a holy man who knew God. The book described the way to spiritual maturity as a holy trade with God, which is:

All of me, none of God
Less of me, more of God
None of me, all of God.

Scripture: *The fear of the Lord is the instruction for wisdom, and before honor comes humility.* (Proverbs 15:33)

The reward of humility and the fear of the Lord are riches, honor and life. (Proverbs 22:4)

...Clothe yourselves with humility toward one another for God is opposed to the proud but gives grace to the humble. (I Peter 5:5)

Prayer: Lord, today I choose Your holy trade. I didn't understand Your love brings humility. As I know You more fully, I feel brave enough to say, "Yes Lord." I give you all the self-words that are part of my life so You can dwell more fully in my heart. Teach me to love as You love through me. I pray a day will come when there is none of me and all of God.

My Revelation:

The Place of Blessings

Like a lily among the thorns, so is My darling among the maidens. **(2:2)**

Prince Charming bathed the maiden in words of affection. Yes, He agreed, she is as a lily, but not a common field flower. She reflects the beauty of a lily, meaning purity.[4]

God always expresses Himself with positive, encouraging, life-giving words of love. I've found He can rebuke me, and though I feel ashamed for failing Him, there is also encouragement. His words of correction impart loving possibilities for constructive change.

With the revelation of God's Word always being life giving, I knew I needed to understand scripture differently. Some of the words in my Bible sounded judgmental and condemning. They didn't agree with the loving Voice I was learning to know. Could the Holy Spirit show me if all scripture is really full of His life and love?

Reading the Word again, I awakened to new understanding of God's heart for people.

When I found a verse that made God sound harsh, I meditated on what Love might really be saying. My question became, *How did God wrap His love around this scripture?* It was always there. Even in the hard places.

Thorns, in this verse, represent offensive people. As the maiden carries the fragrance of God, others experience a whiff of heaven's purity through her life. The Spirit's scent awakens their desire to know the King. Without any understanding, their heads rise to sniff the aroma of her presence, just as in the natural a dog would be curious about the neighbor's unseen barbecue.

When others attack hurtfully, it can be as painful as getting stuck with a thorn. But now, when the maiden is pricked by someone's offense the beautiful fragrance of God flows freely.

Like an apple tree among the trees of the forest, so is my Beloved among the sons. In His shade I took great delight and sat down, and His fruit was sweet to my taste. (2:3)

Before, the maiden's prophetic words explained lying in His bed is like resting in life. Now, another glimpse of His presence is described as sitting under a tree that's continually full of fruit, blossoms, and shiny green leaves. (Revelation 22:2) Our abundant, supernatural God is the Tree of Life.

There is peace and contentment under the protective covering of God (shade). In this wonderful place we are free to taste of His fruit (character).

Taste and see that the Lord is good ... (Psalm 34:8)

She compared His uniqueness to the human race by saying He bears fruit in places where there's only pine trees. He seems gloriously out of place.

As the future bride enjoyed the comfort of the tree's protective covering, their courtship cemented His faithfulness and goodness into her heart. With His continual blessings she came to know the One she loves even more.

This is the same as a wife who knows her husband's character so completely she can figure out almost any surprise he has for her. By the maiden's close relationship with her Beloved, she experienced His faithfulness so fully she can almost guess what amazing thing He'll do next to bless her. She's aware of the delight He finds in giving her the desires of her heart. Pleasure flows as He listens carefully to her requests and answers her prayers.

However, His extravagance in giving so much won't spoil her. Instead, His blessings make her feel whole and secure. He knows her focus is on Him, not gifts. His goodness gave her confidence in the fact He will always faithfully cares for her.

God wants to show His character to His people. When we experience His blessings as He heals our sick bodies, we come to *know* Him as our *Healer*. As He sends resources just in time, we *know* He is our

Provider. He protects us from a terrible car accident and we recognize He is our *Protector.*

He teaches and blesses as we rest under His bountiful tree of provision, protection, and abundance.

Personally, I thought my time of rest in the shade of His blessings meant I was complete and mature. My life changed so much I felt very alive and spiritually grown up. Reveling in His many blessings, I thought God was entirely happy with me. And truly, He was for the moment. Everything was working out abundantly above anything I could ask or think. (Ephesians 3:20)

I had no idea there could be so much more.

Scripture: ... *The Lord is your shade at your right hand* ... (Psalm 121:5)

Taste and see that the Lord is good ... (Psalm 34:8)

Blessed are those who wash their robes, that they may have the right to the tree of life ... (Revelation 22:14)

... Jesus ... has blessed us with every spiritual blessing in the heavenly places in Christ. (Ephesians 1:3)

Prayer: Lord, break through my religious mindset and let me see how You have wrapped Your love around every scripture. Help me be so familiar with Your voice I can quickly recognize anything in my mind that doesn't sound like Your love. Thank You for all Your blessings. I pray I don't take them for granted. Thank You for the privilege of knowing You by Your names, Healer, Provider and Protector.

My Revelation:

The Banquet House

He brought me to the Banqueting Hall, His banner over me is love. (2:4)

The Bridegroom encouraged the maiden until she was ready for a new level of Kingdom life. He took her to the Banqueting House, which can also be translated the House of Wine (delights). The enjoyment of this place of progression is different than the blessings she experienced at the Table of the King. The Banqueting House is reserved for celebrations and entertaining guests, just as we enjoy banquets.

The maiden said yes to His request to leave everything and follow Him. (John 12:26) Her faithfulness indicated her readiness for a deeper commitment to the Groom, so He gave an engagement party for His betrothed. He will also reveal a glimpse of the future He planned for them together. This will encourage her to press into, and receive, all His promises.

While preparing a study on this portion of Song of Solomon, I couldn't understand what He was describing here. Nothing I'd read in books touched my spirit as to what He wanted me to know. Sitting at the computer, I felt as if I was sweating drops of blood to get the explanation the Holy Spirit had for me.

Finally, He spoke, "You've had this experience."

Really? I thought about His words but drew a blank.

"Remember the dream you had where you went into the restaurant with the tinkling of sparkling wine glasses on the tables? That was the House of Wine. Share your dream."

Oh, how I didn't want to reveal my crazy dreams to people. Obedience to a supernatural King never seems to come easy.

In the dream, I was with a realtor (Holy Spirit) shopping for a house. We entered a huge mansion. At one side of the beautiful, expansive foyer stood a row of men and women dressed in crisp black and white uniforms. As we walked by, each servant greeted me formally. The realtor said, "The servants come with the house."

I thought, *This house is way out of my price range.*

We proceeded through a large corridor with huge doors on each side. The realtor opened one of the massive wood entries. Inside was a great banquet room, like one you would see in a spectacular ancient castle. It had a large table in the middle. Groups of people were scattered around the room, chatting and having a celebration.

We moved on and opened the next door. Inside, the same scene was repeated except there were more tables and people. They were having a party and exchanging gifts wrapped in gold.

After seeing other amazing places in the castle, the realtor and I got into a golf cart and headed down a big hill. All the time I was thinking, *I've got to get out of here. This place is way out of my price range.* I looked back for one last glance of the mansion. It was so much larger than I realized. Obviously, we hadn't even begun to see the entire house. I thought to myself, *it would take a lifetime to see all the rooms of this place.* The farther we drove down the hill, the better I could see. The house was spread atop the whole mountain range. More like a city than a home.

We drove by a charming little village. The colorful shops were painted soft blue, coral, yellow and mint green. We passed a bakery, a fruit stand, and a place that sold baskets and flowers. One shop carried dishes and another displayed fine linens.

My realtor said, "All the shops go with the house. They provide for every need and are included in the price."

Get me out of here. What am I doing? A person couldn't afford this place if they worked three lifetimes for a huge salary.

The next thing I knew, my guide suggested lunch, and we parked in front of a restaurant. The building was so different from all the colorful shops. Old dark wood framed stained glass windows. The fragrance of cedar hung in the air. My realtor said the Owner of the house liked this restaurant best. We would join Him.

Stepping inside, we stood together in a small beige cubical. The tiny space was an odd first impression for the lovely old building. Suddenly, the realtor was gone. Where was she? How did she get out? There were no doors or windows in the little room. As I stood wondering what was happening, I glanced up and saw a ladder attached to the high ceiling next to a two-foot hole. Puzzled, I stared in disbelief, but it seemed to be the only possible exit. So, I grabbed hold and pulled myself up to the opening. I stuck one shoulder through the hole, and then the other, thinking, *if this were my place, I'd make a better entrance to get in.* Instantly, Matthew 7:14 came to mind, *Narrow is the way that leads to life and few will find it.*

Pushing through the tiny passage, I stretched up enough to look around. What a sight. The dark hues of rich wood walls set a background for the display of colors dancing in the low light from the reflections of the stained-glass windows. Tables were prepared for a fine banquet where many different wines would be served. Each table setting included six to eight wine glasses. They sparkled in the low flickering candlelight. I heard the cheerful noises of the restaurant. People laughed as they enjoyed conversations and consumed a bounty of heavenly food. Silverware tinkled against the plates and crystal glasses as they touched. It was quite noisy but also pleasant. The musical sounds of the environment reminded me of wind chimes. I gasped in awe at the beautiful scene.

The realtor saw me and said, "Oh, there you are, come and meet the Owner."

Getting up, I dusted off and walked with her to a large booth where He sat. I have no memory of His appearance. He asked how I liked His house. My honest response was, "It is wonderful but far too expensive for me." I began to explain I couldn't afford His property in a thousand lifetimes when He interrupted.

"I don't want you to buy it. I want to give it to you to manage for Me."

Shocked, I fired back, "No one could manage all there is here in a lifetime."

He paused to take a bit of food. Then chewed, swallowed, and casually spoke. "You just say it, and they will do it."

Suddenly, I woke up and thought, *What? He wants to give me all He owns to manage for Him. And who are they?*

I asked, "Lord, who are 'they' who will do anything I speak?"

Complete silence reigned. I waited. No answer. I was expected to believe His words by faith.

I'd often wondered if there was any real meaning to my silly dreams. But people in the Bible had some strange night visions. They asked God for an explanation, and He gave them the needed insight; so I asked too.

The Holy Spirit taught me the wine represented bubbling delight and joy. The guests were the great cloud of witnesses mentioned in Hebrews 12:1 who continually cheer us on. All of heaven is rejoicing as Jesus's bride matures. In my dream, everyone was happy and excited because I'd said yes to all the Lord asked of me.

He wanted me to manage the Kingdom of God by just speaking what needed to be done. Then somehow someone would take care of everything. God's ways are so mysterious.

Soon I realized this was the call of an intercessor. A person who sits with Jesus and prays back to Him whatever He shows them to speak forth.

The call was also to release the voice of a prophet. Prophets listen to hear what God wants to tell them about His plans, then, with the Holy Spirit's anointing, they declare those words to heaven and earth. By the powerful simplicity of a word spoken at the right time, things happen to bring forth God's plans and purposes.

I felt God wanted me to intercede for my city, so I watched what was happening locally. Of course, God was interested in His churches around town. But He was also concerned about the schools, our government, and businesses.

So I prayed.

He makes our assignments so simple. Sometimes my total project for the day took place when I drove by some unholy store and felt God's heart of sadness for those inside. I would ask Jesus to make it go away.

Or I'd drive through an old, worn-out part of the city. By the sadness I felt in my heart, I knew Jesus wanted to resurrect the depressed area and bring life back.

So I prayed.

The most amazing things started to happen. Some of the churches got new pastors. Several new houses of worship opened their doors. People began to see potential in the downtown part of the city. Lovely new shops opened. The beautiful old homes in the rundown neighborhoods were being restored. The unholy store closed.

God gave me the assignment to manage His Kingdom. That seemed impossible. But He also explained how I would accomplish His plan. *They will do it when I speak.* I wonder if we'll ever really grasp the power of our prayers.

The prophetic voice is also powerful. When words are spoken through prophetic authority, angels and demons move with their assignment to either establish God's Kingdom or the enemy's camp. Therefore, our words must always be guarded with purity, humility, and love.

... Death and life are in the power of the tongue ... (Proverbs 18:21)

The Lord's hope is for everyone to join the Spirit at His Banqueting House where overwhelming possibilities await fulfillment. His plans always seem far too challenging to ever be possible. But He has provided everything needed for success.

The privilege of entering the House of Wine with its delights and joy is for those who pursue the fullness of everything God has for them. Intimacy with Jesus, the Bridegroom, opens our hearts to personal supernatural experiences, and divine assignments.

Once we're shown the magnitude of God's Kingdom, and we willingly accept our place in it, He plants His banner of Love over us declaring we belong to Him. Whoever opposes those under the banner of God will be fighting God[1].

Scripture: *And the Lord of hosts will prepare a lavish banquet for all peoples on this mountain; a banquet of aged wine, choice pieces with marrow, and refined, aged wine. And on this mountain He will swallow up the covering that is over all peoples, even the veil that is stretched over all nations. He will swallow up death for all time, and the Lord God will wipe tears away from all faces, and He will remove the reproach of His people from all the earth, for the Lord has spoken. And it will be said in that day, behold, this is our God for whom we have waited that He might save us. ... let us rejoice and be glad in His salvation.* (Isaiah 25:6-9)

Prayer: Is there really a Banqueting House in the Kingdom of God for us? Do You want to have us receive our assignments? If so, Lord I choose to enter. I don't want to miss anything You have for me. Please prepare my heart to live in the fullness of my destiny. I understand whatever You have planned for me will be beyond my abilities; otherwise I wouldn't need You so desperately. I ask for my spirit-eyes to be open. Remove all doubt from me so I can embrace my assignment by faith, without any questions or fear.

My Revelation:

Lovesick

Sustain me with raisin cakes; refresh me with apples, because I am lovesick. (2:5)

Falling in love brings romance and excitement. New life awakens as hope explodes. But love is also active, continually growing until it consumes a heart. It demands fulfillment. If not emotionally satisfied it can feel like being physically sick. Despair and longing overtakes the joy and delight once shared.

When I found love, I remember thinking, *I don't like being in love, it's too painful.* We had fallen in love, were engaged, and planning the wedding, but all we really wanted was to be together. Just a few hours apart made me hurt. How strange something which started out lovely could hurt so much.

Two verses ago, the maiden thought she had it all together. The relationship between the couple was perfect. Then something supernatural happened. Love's passion found new depths. Once she accepted the King's life of royalty with His commitment of *forever love,* her passion grew until she was overcome, lovesick. All she wanted was to be with the One she loved.

With the privilege of the Banquet House she was stretched by the impossibility of her God-sized assignment. The reality of her future with Him created feelings of weakness, being disoriented, and totally undone.

So as the maiden and I experienced His manifest presence, we cried, "Sustain me, I'm lovesick." We loved Him enough to do whatever He asked, but we needed His strength (raisins cakes) and the continual refreshment of His sweetness (apples[8]).

For me, God was ready to convey how much I pushed His love away. When I finally surrendered and allowed Him to possess me, I found what I'd always wanted. His pure, holy, life-giving love set me free to trust the One who filled my heart. I knew He would keep me safe, so I wasn't afraid to be vulnerable with Him.

Perfect love casts out all fear ... (I John 4:18)

The more time the maiden spent with the Beloved, the more personal He became. She found His character and personality to be divine perfection. Each quality of His life was so extravagant and powerful, they became His names. He is known as Grace, Love, Goodness, Mercy, Kindness, and much more.

Fortunately, she also came to know Him as Gentle because if He embraced her more than slightly with His all-powerful passion, she would probably be destroyed.

The God who lifts up the islands like fine dust (Isaiah 40:15) has taken a personal interest in His maiden, and breathed a declaration of His commitment to their future together.

His left hand is under my head and His right hand embraces me. (2:6)

The maiden asked for His strength in her weakness. In answer, He took her in His arms. As He held her He also answered her prayer to see Him face to face. He said, "Seek my face," and she obeyed. (Psalm 27:8-9)

The one the Lord loves rest between His shoulders. (Deuteronomy 33:12)

The Spirit's embrace brings supernatural strength, health, and restoration. This is similar to a husband's arms around his wife when her world seems to fall apart. Or, it would be as comforting as a parent holding a child close to ease the pain of not making the team. Their hug helps put all the broken pieces of our heart back together again.

Scripture: *Look to the Lord and His strength; seek His face always.* (I Chronicles 16:11)

Blessed are the pure in heart for they shall see God. (Matthew 5:8)

... My grace is sufficient for you, for My power is perfected in weakness ... (II Corinthians 12:9)

Prayer: Lord, I need to feel Your embrace. I'm weak and undone, needing strength and refreshing. Please help me relax, surrender, and allow You to possess me with life-giving love. I want to trust You enough to be vulnerable to Your supernatural touch. Can I really see You face to face? I chose to experience the pain of being lovesick for You?

My Revelation:

Do Not Awaken Until She Desires

I adjure you, O daughters of Jerusalem, that you will not arouse or awaken My love, until she desires. (2:7)

The King told the daughters the maiden is lovesick and she must rest. In His arms she found the Sabbath rest of God.

For the one who enters His rest has himself rested from his works as God did from His. (Hebrews 4:10)

The bride laid down her personal plans and found *freedom from self.* While in a time of relaxation and trust, the Holy Spirit went deep into her soul and worked like a miner, opening new areas within her where He would make His home.

The places of our spirit-man are bigger and deeper than human size. This revelation came alive to me one evening when a pastor prayed with me. The powerful presence of God came, and I melted to the floor. Supernatural currents of energy flowed through me. The experience was awesome. As joy engulfed me, I started laughing out loud. I mean *loud.* There I was, lying on the floor rolling back and forth, roaring with laughter. Normally, I would have been embarrassed showing such a display of emotion, but this experience was too wonderful. I was having so much fun I didn't care who heard me, or what others were doing. I thought, *I'm rolling on the floor. I've never seen a holy roller before.* I laughed all the more. God's joy felt bigger than I am. The delight was above my head, all the way down to my toes and out as if I was over ten feet tall.

Finally quieting down, while still lying on the floor, I asked the Lord for understanding. What happened to me? How was it possible to feel an expanse of emotion so huge it felt larger than my body?

The Holy Spirit opened my understanding. We are much more than our flesh appears. Amazing power and authority dwells in us which has never been tried. One spirit-led human is powerful enough to change the world. Our spirit isn't confined to the size of our body or meant to be controlled by our flesh. We were created to live in the Spirit, not in the limitations of physical humanity.

This concept stretched me in places I didn't know existed. The Holy Spirit was enlarging the *deep* places of my spirit where *Deep* calls. (Psalm 42:7) He was doing a profound spiritual work because I was finally willing.

God *stretches our tent pegs and enlarges our borders* ... (Isaiah 54:2)

When our spirit-eyes are open, we experience supernatural visions, which can be similar to watching television in our mind, or as simple as a quick picture or a short scene.

Today, we're bombarded with so many images it's easy to miss the precious pictures God wants to share. Imagine years ago when David, as a shepherd boy, had no distractions but a flock of sheep. He captured his majestic visions of God in song and they were shared in Psalms.

As the Holy Spirit taught me to see unseen things, I began to recognize little visions were messages from my Beloved. Through a group of quick mental videos, He revealed what He did in my life the night on the floor.

In the first vision I was inside a dark cave. A wet, muddy path wove through it. He was allowing me to see the condition of my soul.

I heard in my spirit, "New uncharted territory where no one has ever entered."

Later, I saw the same cave, but this time strings of lights were everywhere. The mud was dry, and the cave was clean and ready to be used.

The next time I saw the scene the caverns were even drier and bright with light, as if it were a sunbaked desert in a cave. The scene was so real I felt hot, dry air blowing.

The last time I saw the cave I knew the Holy Spirit was flooding the empty dry places of what appeared to be a winding riverbed. Great gushes of

Living Water flushed through the caves of my soul. It became a mighty bubbling underground river sweeping through curves inside me, splashing from side to side.

This is what He did for me as I laid on the floor laughing and rolling. New, unknown places within my soul were prepared to open. That night my cleansed soul filled with the Living Water of God.

I've heard a mysterious phrase to explain some of the things God does. *He takes us deeper to go higher.* Sounds silly, but it's true. As the Spirit revealed the deep places within me He was filling, I had no idea they were creating a path for soaring into new heights of the Spirit realm.

While the maiden rests, the Holy Spirit is stretching and opening new areas within her. He has gone deep into her soul to liberate her so she can fly with Him.

Scripture: *The King is present; therefore, be still.* (Habakkuk 2:20)

... The Lord will quiet you with His love ... (Zephaniah 3:17)

Those that wait upon the Lord will renew their strength. They will mount up with wings of eagles, they will run and not be weary, they will walk and not faint. (Isaiah 40:31)

Look to the Lord and His strength; seek His face always. (I Chronicles 16:11)

Prayer: Lord, help me yield to the profound work You desire to accomplish in my life. I lay down my personal plans. I repent of small thinking and choose to know the majesty of my God who is love. I welcome You to take me deeper into the Spirit's call. Free me to soar the heights of Your Spirit realm. Stretch my tent pegs and enlarge my borders (Isaiah 54:2) to create more room for Your glory to reign in my life. Help me learn how to be quiet so I can have the knowledge of Your presence more fully.

My Revelation:

The Dance in the Spirit

Listen! My Beloved! Behold, He is coming, climbing on the mountains, leaping on the hills! (2:8)

The maiden described an open vision. Her Beloved has no limitations. He can instantly be moving about earth and reveal Himself, or living in what she called mountains, which represent the high places of the kingdom of God.

While in rest, yet continually learning, the Holy Spirit taught me obedience brings the privilege of knowing the timing and rhythm of God's Kingdom. This movement could be compared to the steps of a dance. The Lord drew, and I came closer. He said, "Wait here," and I learned to pause. In those few moments, a door of opportunity would open to speak words of life to someone. I found a delay of three minutes kept me from being in the car accident I passed. This is what I call the supernatural dance of life. Truly, every day is full of God's call to follow Him (dance) into His Kingdom destiny for our lives.

When we learn there is only a veil between us and God's Spirit Kingdom we will know even more pleasure.

While alone with my Beloved I've experienced dancing with the Spirit. As I worshiped my awakened spirit became aware of His presence.

In those times with Him I felt my King wanted me to dance for Him as part of worshiping. The Trinity finds such abandonment irresistible.

By faith, as I worshiped, I moved around. Then surprisingly, I stepped into His embrace. In the Spirit we became a couple whirling about in divine, rapturous expressions of love. As I yielded to Him in the dance we seemed to lift off the floor twirling freely in the heavens. Then, ever so gently, He brought me back in earth's reality.

As I learned His rhythm, I realized once He's allowed to lead, the dance of His presence continues day and night. Even in complete rest, with no conscious awareness of anything, the beat goes on. In dreams, He teaches and stretches with new ideas too big to grasp while awake.

I wanted nothing more than to stay in *The Dance of the Spirit*. When I woke in the morning, I tried to focus on anything I was meant to learn through my dreams. I listened for the morning song in my heart. Sometimes God gives us songs if we have ears to hear. He is never silent in His love for us, so I asked for songs. He answers my desire with love songs, or a hymn of worship, or even a musical message for my day. So, if on awakening you wonder why you're humming music from way back when, review the words. God might be giving His thoughts or special directions for the day. He is talking. We just need to take time to listen.

The Holy Spirit became my best friend. In the rhythm of life I trusted Him to plan my schedule. Even while shopping, He knows what I'd like, and where the bargains can be found. Sometimes, I've walked into a store just as the sale signs went up. It's all part of the Spirit's dance.

In the balance of life's dance He might say, "No more chasing Me today. Go and play; and I really mean play. Be a child with your children. Have fun with your husband." This is also part of the rhythm and obedience of the timing of the dance of God in two realms.

I was learning to understand what the scripture meant when it said walk in the steps of the Spirit.

Scripture: *Since we live by the Spirit let us keep in step with the Spirit.* (Galatians 5:25)

A man's steps are directed by the Lord ... (Proverbs 20:24)

... walk by the Spirit, and you will not carry out the desire of the flesh. (Galatians 5:16)

... Besides Thee, I desire nothing on earth. (Psalm 73:25)

He who is faithful in a very little thing is faithful also in much ... (Luke 16:10)

Prayer: Lord, sometimes You feel close enough for us to dance. Help me keep in step with Your Spirit. Fine-tune my inner hearing so I will know it is You speaking in things as simple as shopping, reaching out to people, or even making a phone calls. Let every step be led by You. I choose to be faithful in the little things so You can trust me with more. Remind me to play and have fun. I will listen for Your songs in the mornings, and the message You have for my day?

My Revelation:

Hidden Hindrances

Behold He stands behind our wall; He is looking through the windows, gazing through the lattice. (2:9)

During rest, the maiden gained new strength as her Beloved wooed her with holy passion. In His gentle way, He looked into the window of her soul, longing for her to be free, but for now, He must remain behind her walls.

Purity has made its home within her, so at this point the Holy Spirit desired to go deeper into her hidden emotions. He longed to bring life where pain remained. Jesus knows the hindrances of our past devastations.

As the maiden surrendered to the Lord's deeper work, He dredged up memories that were hard to face. Strong, deep-seated emotions buried in her soul. He wanted to be given permission to enter where shame and fear guarded the doors of her heart. The time had come for her to face the hardest memories of her life.

At this time she couldn't acknowledge past trauma held any power over her. In reality, it defined who she was. Even negative, hurtful things made her someone. So, she faced a spiritual crisis. If she gave Him possession of her past, she would be different. There's fear in change. A crisis question rang in her mind, "Who would I be if I'm no longer a victim?"

Hope took a seat in her heart. Who *would* she be? Is freedom possible?

In the intensity of out-of-this-world love, God asked permission to go into the rooms of her soul. She didn't realize she was holding anything back. In fact, she was so sure she had given Him everything she called the wall *our wall*.

The Beloved knew the maiden was now strong enough to deal with the ghosts of the past.

Divine transformation comes through freedom from negative emotions and memories. If she allows it, the Holy Spirit will replace each stronghold with Kingdom emotions and thoughts.

Notice how far their love-affair and her maturing have come, before the Holy Spirit is free to deal with the negative roots in her heart.

Love is ready to ask for some hard things. It takes bravery to face the past. He wants her to bring darkness to light by giving Him her secrets, hurts, pain, disappointments, devastations, scars and hate. He longs to be given every ugly thing still holding her captive.

She didn't know it was possible to give her dark past to such Holiness. The maiden felt, if He knew about her dark side, she would be disqualified to be His bride. All she can do in her unworthiness is yield to this new request by saying, *Yes Lord.*

Love is the key that brings freedom to what seems impossible.

With her permission, He revealed the deep painful memories of the night her dad left. Just a child, she loved him so much. She always questioned, "If I'd been a better child, would he have stayed?" As if our soul has rooms, this one was owned by rejection and filled with loss. Jesus was asking to enter and destroy those negative, locked away emotions. When she agrees He will encompass her with the Father's love as He unlatches her heart, and fills it with His adoring acceptance and love.

The wall could be the emotional secret of the abortion others forced her to have. She was so young. That room has haunted her too long. In the deep recesses of her soul she bares scars that don't heal. They seep with pain, holding her hostage.

The room yells out, "Unworthy," when she wants to get close to Jesus. He longs to be allowed to destroy the tormenting oppression, and restore the void left by her loss. The Holy Spirit is ready to decorate the walls in the barren room with new décor. He will paint them with unconditional love. His fragrance of life will purify the stench of death in the air. For color and fun the furnishings will be His abundant fruitfulness.

Another wall could be *infidelity*. This room hides the names of people she gave her heart and body to, other than her mate. Voices call out reminding her of indiscretions when there's the nudge to be a spiritual leader. She is hopelessly locked in her past, and feels as if her heart's in pieces. The Holy Spirit wants entry. He can remove the soul ties that shattered her heart, and made it hard to trust anyone. Love's glue will put her back together as it creates wholeness and restoration so she can be His virgin bride. *Old things will pass away and all things become new.* (II Corinthians 5:17)

The enemy gains power when he convinces us to keep our stuff concealed in darkness. Freedom comes when hidden things are brought to light.

Secrets may hide what a relative did to her as a child. Shameful, unspeakable things have been buried deep inside. Jesus wants permission to go in with His holy light to remove the power darkness has to destroy her destiny. Childhood will be supernaturally restored, bringing hope and the liberty to trust and fully love.

As the future bride allowed the Holy Spirit to flow in all the undisclosed places of her heart, she experienced freedom from shame and fear.

Shedding those dark memories and emotions felt as if she took off a confining, heavy robe. The encumbrance of shame no longer binds her feet. She feels light and free as she steps into new life. With newfound freedom, progression has taken place. Her Beloved stood behind her walls. Now the walls are gone. New abilities flow freely as she lives *in Him*. Earth's limitations can no longer hold her back.

Her future will be full of unexplainable experiences, mysteries requiring courage and a spirit of adventure. God has prepared her for a *walk of naked faith*. This comes from knowing His character so well she trusts Him more than anything she sees, feels, or experiences.

Scriptures: *For nothing is hidden, except to be revealed, nor has anything been secret, but that it should come to light.* (Mark 4:22).

Violence will not be heard again in your land ... (Isaiah 60:18)

Be strong, and let your heart take courage all you who hope in the Lord. (Psalm 31:24)

Prayer: Lord, today I give You the secrets hidden deep in my heart. I know they are a hindrance in my ability to receive Your love completely. I can't imagine what it will be like to live without the torment of my past. Again I say, "Yes Lord." I choose to give You even more of myself today, including all shame, guilt, and even the things I've forgotten. I don't want anything to hinder the liberty of fully knowing You. Thank You for new life.

My Revelation:

Come Away

My Beloved spoke and said to me, arise my darling, my beautiful one, and come away. For Behold, the winter is past, the rain is over and gone. Flowers appear on the earth; the season of singing has come ... Arise, come My darling, My beautiful one, and come with Me. (2:10-13)

As if asleep while in surgery, the maiden yielded to the hands of the Great Physician. Her haunted, tormenting past was as deadly and destructive as a physical disease when it attacks our body. The poison emotions in her heart are gone and she's healed. Even the scars have been removed.

The Beloved wanted her to recognize her new freedom and liberty. He declared more ownership as He called her *My* darling, *My* beautiful one. What lovely words to hear as she woke up.

God called her to rest. In reality, several years could have passed before He urged her to awaken. He also asked her to *come away* to His Kingdom. He said, "Come live in My house, and be a part of what I'm doing. I want you to realize you can speak to chains that bind people, and they will fall off. Come be with Me as I raise a standard of righteousness over nations. Let Me show you our victory as lies and deception are cast into utter darkness. Enjoy the sight of Truth ringing crystal clear throughout the earth. Come be a part of My plans." (Psalm 85:11)

This place of transition in a Christian's walk is enormous. During her rest, the maiden matured in humility. With this virtue she feels no need to prove her worth. Pride doesn't try to push her to be the best or to strive for the heights of success. While she was embraced in the Beloved's presence, she learned to appreciate quietness and contentment.

But there is no standing still in the race she entered. And now no walls hold her back. She has new abilities in the Spirit to freely climb mountains and leap in the high places. She has acclimated to pure Kingdom air, and has clear vision of the spirit realm.

Winter, where everything seemed dead, is over. Through the dormant time, the maiden's root system went deep into the strength and nourishment of the Holy Spirit, as He filled all the empty places of her free soul with Himself.

Her capacity for true pleasure has awakened her senses. Love brings new delight. She knows the joy of spring's promises of new life. A gentle breeze touching her neck as it passes fills her with the wonder of being fully alive physically and spiritually. Everything is more vibrant than ever before. The sky is bluer and the grass is greener. A ripple in a pool is mesmerizing. Even the shapes of leafs on the trees and bushes are fascinating. We would say she takes time to stop and smell the roses as she embraces life. God has given her new ability to hear. The melodies of birds capture her ears with delightful fascination. Children playing create musical sounds. Liberty has put a new song of gratitude in her heart as she relishes freedom. She moves with the music of the breeze, and listens to the melody of a babbling brook. For the first time she can remember, her heart is free. Her spirit joins the birds in song. *She sings.*

The maiden sees the Spirit Kingdom and recognizes *the wide places* (Psalms 18:19, Psalms 31:8) of freedom the Bridegroom has prepared.

God is so gentle, patient, and kind. This is the second time He called her to come away. Knowing how weak His bride is, God has unfathomable patience. He willingly calls again and again using His positive love language with words such as *My darling, My beautiful one.* God never holds back His gushy words of affection which reveal His desire for us.

Scriptures: *Sing for joy to God our strength: shout joyfully to God ...* (Psalm 81:1)

O Come, let us sing for joy to the Lord! Let us shout joyfully to the rock of our salvation. Let us come before His presence with thanksgiving; let us shout joyfully to Him with psalms for the Lord is a great God ... (Psalm 95:1-3 NKJ)

I will sing to the Lord as long as I live; I will sing praise to my God while I have my being.
(Psalm 104:33)

It was for freedom that Christ set us free; therefore keep standing firm and do not be subject again to a yoke of slavery. (Galatians 5:1)

You shall know the truth, and the truth shall make you free. (John 8:32)

Prayer: Lord, Thank You for freedom. Thank You for a new song in my heart. Thank You for the joy of being alive and awakened to Your Kingdom reality. I love feeling loved. I invite You to do something today that will make me laugh. You're so much fun. I will sing Your praises all day long.

My Revelation:

The Secret Place

O My dove, that art in the clefts of the rock, (the secret places of the stairs) (2:14)

Earlier, the maiden was described as having eyes of a dove. (1:15) Now the Bridegroom expresses His affection by calling her a dove. Peace and loyalty have become her character.

He's delighted with the transitions she allowed as she followed Him from the vineyard, to the Table of Blessing, then to the House of Wine, His Verdant Bed, and the Apple Tree.

In this verse, the Holy Spirit is telling her she has moved again. Her new address is the *Clefts of the Rock*. A cleft is an indented formation in a wall. Exodus 33:22 says, *When My glory passes by, I will put you in a cleft in the Rock and cover you with My hand until I have passed by.* Jesus has become her single-focus and her Rock of protection.

Her spirit continually yields to His loving persuasion as the Holy Spirit orchestrates her life. She wasn't aware of her advancement when she reached the secret stairs hidden in the mountainside that led to the fullness of God. Who could have guessed there was such a place?

Madame Guyan said, *Your spirit ascends to God by giving itself up to the annihilating power of Divine Love.*[3]

We have the privilege of giving our life to God's divine love. What are we waiting for?

In this secret place, the bride will come to know the Holy Spirit personally. He's no longer *The* Holy Spirit as if only a whiff of smoke. Now, He is *Holy Spirit*, third person of the Trinity. He has become her wise mentor, training her how to live as supernatural royalty. She knows Him as a precious friend and faithful confidant. He is always encouraging yet continually presses her toward perfection. His character is very gentle and kind, but He will make her miserable if she tries to stay content with less than His best. In love, He never gives up on her, even though she might feel hopeless about herself.

Coming to The Secret Place with God is by invitation only. *Many are called but few are chosen* (Matt. 22:14). Everything must be laid down to enter the Holy Mountain of God.

The Cleft of the Rock (Jesus) is the short cut between two realms. The stairs are a place of ascension where no ordinary man can reach.[4] The supernatural path leads from earth to God's Throne Room. Only those free and able to see with spirit-eyes will find their way.

The stairs were promised to Nathanael when he was told *he would see the heavens opened and the angels of God ascending and descending on the Son of Man.* (John 1:51)

I was shown this flight of steep, stone-hewn stairs inside a split in a mountain. One of God's names was on each step. Jesus's words came to mind, *"If my name be lifted up I will draw all men to myself.* (John 12:32)

As I climbed the stairs, I stepped on the word *Grace.* I would stay on that step for a while. Learning to know Jesus as grace crushed me, leaving me with the reality of my desperate need for a grace-filled life. When I was allowed to step on wisdom, I was overwhelmed with the magnitude of our enlightened God. I longed to know even a portion of what it is to be wise.

The stairs are the place where the bride comes to truly *know* the Godhead by Their character, virtues, and names. Each step brings deeper and higher revelation of who God really is. This knowledge will probably challenge us forever.

Amazingly, I also found when I was willing to take another somewhat frightening, unknown, steep step I was sometimes whisked, as if on wings, into the Throne Room for an audience with the King.

The overwhelming presence of the Lord on this spiritual mountain brings reverent, trembling, holy fear. But, at the same time, there's exhilarating elation in being with Him to enjoy the pleasure of His all-consuming presence.

The experience of God encompassing His child is what Moses knew when he was on the mountain. God's glorious power on Moses's face glowed so brightly he had to wear a covering to meet with the people. (Exodus 34:29)

Show Me your face, let Me hear your voice; for your voice is sweet, and your face is lovely. **(2:14)**

A new day has come. The maiden experienced a personal visitation from her God-man, and she knows the reality of the shortcut between two realms. After dying to self, which felt as if it took forever, she's now on fast-forward.

The Beloved spoke His adoring words as He asked to see her face. He was checking to make sure she was alright after the disruption of moving deeper into the heights of His Spirit. This change would be, in a very tiny way, similar to moving from sea level in Florida, to the high altitudes of the Colorado mountaintops where the air is very thin.

God's Kingdom atmosphere and earth environment are very different. The Glory Realm is vibrant with life and energy. Love radiates as powerful as the sun on a bright summer day. So, in this verse, He wants to make sure her spirit is adjusting to the heights of the journey that has taken her to the Throne of the God of the Universe. He watched her, as His betrothed leaned forward enticed by the rich words of majestic angels worshiping around the Throne. The glorious sounds of heaven's praise ring forth as loud chaos. Millions of voices sang their own worship songs, all at the same time. Yet somehow there was perfect harmony and order. The music reverberates from mountain to mountain sending out rapturous expressions of affection that doesn't fade away. Echoes upon echoes of adoration fill the atmosphere. Oh, how she longs to express her feelings for her Beloved in such a way.

The Holy Spirit agrees, wanting to loose her voice. She yields to Him, singing melody and words by His leading. As she continues to sing, her worship becomes deeper and richer, filled with Kingdom love and abandonment. The magnificent Words from her Bible come to mind and are magnified as if alive. Yes, truly living words. Waves of worship flow through her body, agreeing with David's prayer to *magnify the Lord with me.* (Psalm 34:3)

There is no hindrance in finding expression as the Holy Spirit leads. She understands the truth of John 4:24 which says, *True worshipers will worship the Father in Spirit and Truth, for they are the kind of worshipers the Father seeks. God is Spirit and His worshipers must worship in Spirit and in Truth.*

The maiden yields, learns, and practices. As she sings the angels join in. She becomes so lost in worship, the angels pause and stand in awe of her powerful devotion.

She becomes a *Worshiper*.

Scripture: ... *Narrow is the way that leads to life and few will find it.* (Matthew 7:14)

... *I will set them securely on high because they know My name.* (Psalm 91:14)

Ascribe to the Lord the glory due to His name. Worship the Lord in holy array. (Psalm 29:2)

All the earth will worship Thee, and will sing praises to Thy name. (Psalm 66:4)

Prayer: Lord, Thank You for the privilege of entering the Cleft of the Rock just as Moses did. I boldly ask to enter, longing to know You better with each step. What an adventure! I ask, Lord, for You to let me hear the sounds of heaven so I can learn to be a worshiper in spirit and in truth. Show me how to acclimate to the Kingdom's air. What amazing requests. I'm realizing how small earth's trials really are in Your grand scheme of things. Thank You.

Little Foxes

Catch for us the foxes, the little foxes that ruin the vineyards, our vineyards that are in bloom. **(2:15)**

Foxes (little tormenters) come into lives to find anything they can chew on. They look for new spiritual growth (young tender vines) ready to bear fruit (blossoms) for the Kingdom. They search for openings in our spiritual armor, which would be little hindrances so normal we don't recognize they are part of us, unless Wisdom and Holiness revealed them.

After giving God everything I could, I began to notice my words. I would say, way too often, "I just hate that." It would be something as simple as hating cold weather, or hating I forgot something.

The Holy Spirit asked, "How can a heart full of love hate anything?"

Ouch! I repented and asked for a guard over my words so I wouldn't say hate. This is the way we catch the little foxes. Each time a word was on my tongue that was the opposite of love, the Holy Spirit would remind me not to speak. With His help I was able to break the habit.

Listening to my own conversation revealed what was in my heart because it's *out of the heart the mouth speaks.* (Matthew 12:34) Negative, critical words had to go. And no more griping.

Whatever is true, whatever is honorable, whatever is right, whatever is pure, whatever is lovely, whatever is of good report, if there is any excellence and if anything worthy of praise, let your mind dwell on these things. (Philippians 4:8)

A saint's mouth is too powerful to speak negative ungodly things into existence.

Death and life are in the power of the tongue. (Proverbs 18:21)

After practicing guarding the words of my mouth, I received a new challenge from the Lord. It was the first of January when He decided my New Year resolution should be I wouldn't have a negative thought all year. He wanted me to think the positive, life-giving things He thinks.

I was to catch the little foxes that flipped through my mind totally unnoticed. The Holy Spirit took guard over my mind, and actually it went pretty well. As I recognized negative thinking, I quickly changed the words to something positive.

The real challenge came the day we were at the golf course ready to play one of my few annual games. As we walked up to the first tee box, the Lord said, "Don't forget, not one negative thought."

What? How was I ever going to think positively as I beat the ground with my golf club? It was quite a test.

Then there were the little fox that ran through my mind when anyone told me they loved me. My response was always, *They don't really love me. They're just saying that.*

The Holy Spirit helped me realize I was rejecting the love He wanted to give me through other people. Little foxes were stealing my joy and feelings of acceptance. I decided to quit listening to the lie. Instead, I'd believe people when they expressed their affection for me.

I announced to my husband I finally believed he loved me. He was pleased and had fun testing me with his admiration. My new response was, "I know you do." He seemed happier with those words than when I spoke words of love to him.

The next fox revealed was when the Holy Spirit said I'd seared my heart. I couldn't imagine such a thing. I've never been one to watch gross things on television or in the movies, or read scary books, so I questioned how such a thing was possible.

He responded, "From watching the news on television. You've seen pictures of war, famine, murders, and devastation until your heart is seared."

It was true. I *could* watch tragedies around the world with very little emotion. Little foxes were destroying my sensitivity to care about the pain of others.

This verse tells us the maiden has spent some time on a fox hunt. If we watched her search, we'd know she took her newfound authority over the little pests in her spiritual garden very seriously. If we saw her, she would look like a woman beating rodents with a broom to get them away from her harvest.

Scripture: *Be renewed in the spirit of your mind.* (Ephesians 4:23)

Gird your mind for action ... (I Peter 1:13)

...*We have the mind of Christ.* (I Corinthians 2:16)

Prayer: Lord, I ask You to fine-tune my mind to catch the little foxes which aren't part of You and holiness. My request is for an excellent mind that is pure and loving. Put a guard over my mouth, and reveal the attitudes of my heart. Help my mind dwell on what is true, honorable, pure, lovely, excellent, praiseworthy, and of good report.

Doubt

My Beloved is mine and I am His; He browses among the lilies. Until the daybreaks and the shadows flee, turn, my Beloved, and be like a gazelle or like a young stag on the mountains of Bether. **(2:16-17)**

The maiden chased foxes away. With spirit-eyes open, she could see the Beloved walking in the garden of her soul while He enjoys her established purity (lilies). She declared the progress of their love relationship. She lives in Him and He lives in her. Over time, as transition took place, the Beloved became her Lover. If she'd written Song of Solomon, she would have put *The End* after verse sixteen. What more could there be? Their partnership has brought sheer fulfillment. Finding contentment in Him, she wants to remain in this present ecstasy forever.

But we know God never leaves us where He finds us. He is always saying, "Come away, My beloved, there's more." He has never-ending Kingdom adventures for those who heed His call. So the Holy Spirit, knowing her perfection must be completed, pulls again with His supernatural force.

In full assurance of their partnership, she told her Lover to turn from her. Perhaps, He has more mountain-leaping to do. Feeling there couldn't be anything more to want or need, she'll be happy to wait for Him in this perfect place.

Out of the maiden's prophetic mouth, the Holy Spirit had her use the words *until the day breaks* (until tomorrow) and *shadows flee* (reflections of sin). These phrases reveal the hindrances keeping her from knowing the fullness of life in the Kingdom of God.

She is beautiful and pure, but perhaps similar to when we sit in a lovely, clean house. When the sun shines through the windows the light reveals tiny bits of dust on the furniture and floating in the air.

The Son's holiness beamed on His bride, bringing with it new possibilities. But the enemy is always around, like dust, to try her with what she perceives as imperfections (shadows). Shadows are illusions. Not reality. At least she doesn't describe herself as dark anymore (1:5).

She is totally cleansed by Jesus's blood, but phantoms lie to her. Deep-rooted *Fear of the Unknown* hinders. The Holy Spirit is at work to help her know *Truth*.

We shouldn't be surprised by the maiden. She's just like all humanity. Jesus fed five thousand people, but shortly after, the disciples doubted.

(Matthew 16:9-10) Peter walked on water, but got wet when doubt raised its ugly head. (Matthew 14:30) The Israelites ate manna for forty years. They were protected by a glory cloud and a pillar of fire, yet they failed over and over because doubt came along. (Numbers 14:27) They experienced God's miracles, but still wanted to go back to Egypt where things were familiar.

The bride has also seen amazing things. However, when all is said and done, she thinks, *"I'll settle for what I know."*

The little word *doubt*, though it seems as simple as a shadow and as elusive as dust, is the enemy's stronghold against maturing in faith.

The maiden didn't realize there would be loss if she didn't go with the Lord. She thought she could be satisfied with their current relationship. Her prophetic words asked the Lord to go to the mountains of Bether, which means separation.[4] Basically our bride put on the brakes. Just as many great romances, when the reality of the changes required for a greater commitment in their relationship is recognized, doubt and fear have a chance to test the commitment.

Do you see the way she stopped moving to the rhythm of the Spirit? He seemed to change the music of their dance from a waltz to perhaps a samba, and she didn't think she could move to the new beat. She has only learned one way to dance.

The Bridegroom wants His bride to have mature faith. Fear and doubt aren't to have any power over her. Her love for Him is to overcome those two hindrances until everything else looks like hate in comparison. (Luke 14:26)

Faith and fear are opposites.
Faith and love grow together as breasts.
Perfect love casts out all fear. (I John 4:18)

One of the challenges to our Christian maturity is, even after we've conquered hindering areas in our lives, the tormentors of the past always circle back to see if there's any opening in our lives for entry. (Matthew 12:43-46) I've noticed they especially challenge us just before God opens new exciting opportunities. The Holy Spirit allows these aggravations to stretch our faith. We are meant to stand our ground and believe God for more than we've known before.

Just as the maiden wanted to rest in her safe comfy place, we know it's easier to stay where we are than to step into new unknown challenges.

Yesterday, as I was preparing this book for publishing, I realized while reading this chapter again, God had me write these words in the past, for now. Today, the bride of Christ is in a new time of transition, just as I am personally. I feel the supernatural pull of the Spirit and hear Him saying, "Come away. Sell all your goods and follow Me."

Yes, right now I'm being stretched to believe for something I can't see or understand. We've experienced this type of transition successfully several times. It should be easy. But just about the time I'm convinced to do exactly what we think we're hearing, I'm filled with doubt. We can't come back to our lovely home if we sell it. What if there's nothing out there for us. We haven't received clear direction on where we're to go.

Reading this chapter again, I laughed. The Lord put this reminder here for me to recognize again the power doubt has to hold us back from His exciting adventures. Perhaps we could stay in comfort the rest of our lives, but we might miss the fulfillment of what is promised in Jeremiah 29:11.

... For I know the plans I have for you, declares the Lord, plans for welfare and not for calamity, to give you a future and a hope.

We don't know what the future looks like right now, but the verse says *He* knows the plans He has for us. We are to willingly follow His leading, sometimes blindly, with trust and faith, free to enjoy the surprises that come with our obedience.

Repenting for allowing doubt to torment me, I chose to trust and have faith in His plans. Immediately, flashes of God's faithfulness over the years whizzed through my mind, as if I were watching a preview of a movie. Joy flooded my heart as doubt took flight, and the truth of God always being faithful, came to rest.

Later in the day while driving, I saw a beautiful red fox dead at the edge of the road. At first, I felt sad seeing such a lovely creature had been killed. Then I heard the Spirit said, "The fox is dead." Thinking about the revelation of the words I'd just heard, I burst into laughter. *The fox is dead. Thank you. Thank you, Lord. Doubt, as a little fox in my life, is dead. I'm free. God, You are so good and so faithful. I'll press in to find Your plans without fear or doubt. You have never failed us yet. Thanks for my pretty red fox lesson.*

Scripture: *... I want every man in every place to pray lifting up holy hands without wrath and doubt.* (I Timothy 2:8)

There is no fear in love, but perfect love casts out fear, because fear involves punishment, and the one who fears is not perfected in love. (I John 4:18)

Prayer: Lord, I repent of being immature in faith, and for leaving room for fear and doubt to torment me. Set me free from fear of the unknown. Help me grow in boldness so I can fully live my Kingdom adventure with You. Help me recognize when You change the rhythm of our dance. Please give me wisdom and maturity to use the prophetic gift You've given me. Reveal the little foxes in my life so I can repent and quickly give those things to You, even when they are pretty little foxes. Help me, Lord Jesus, to have open hands yielded to You. Thank You, for helping me recognize the fact tormentors of the past often return to test where victories have already been won. They want the ground they once controlled back because You are about to do something wonderful. Fill me with Your vision and discernment for the next step.

My Revelation:

The Pursuit

When humility (which is coming to the end of self) reigns, Jesus will be standing right in front of us with His arms open wide, ready to embrace.

When you seek Me with all your heart you will find Me. (Jeremiah 29:13)

All night long on my bed I looked for the one my heart loves; I looked for Him but did not find Him. (3:1)

Desperation for God is a treasure in His Kingdom.

Madame Guyon said, *When the Bridegroom is most drawn to us, He flees from us with what seems the greatest cruelty. Here is love's cruelty. For without such cruel love we would never leave ourselves. We would never come to know what it's like to be lost in God.*[3]

The maiden longed for her Lover, she discovered the heavenly realm was wooing her, even pulling her forward like the draw of a divine magnet, past the veil of humanness into the Spirit of God.

I will get up now and go about the city, through its streets and squares; I will search for the One my heart loves. So I looked for Him but did not find Him. **(3:2)**

In desperation, the future bride headed for the streets to find her Beloved. How strange. She knew He was a mountain-leaping, hill-jumping Lover, so why would she look for Him in the town squares?

The answer. She was still seeking for Him as if He were in the physical realm, not in an invisible realm.

Cities and streets represent places where we communicate. She repeated her practices that once brought the Lord's presence. Things like prayer, worship, fasting, and fellowship with the saints, but nothing changed.

I looked for Him but didn't find Him. Such sad words. She thought she understood everything needed for a close relationship with her Lover, but none of the old patterns worked anymore. Finally, in helpless frustration she came to the end of herself.

The watchmen found me as they made their rounds in the city. And I said, "Have you seen the One my heart loves?" **(3:3)**

Watchmen represent God's shepherds. In the past, they helped the maiden find her Beloved, but she hadn't sought them out this time. Instead, while at their duties, the shepherds spotted the maiden. She hoped they would help.[4]

Again, we're reminded we find encouragement in knowing others are seeking their Lover too. Wisdom and strength come by having other people in our lives. They often give us a different point-of-view, which can possibly help clear up our concerns.

Without all of us working together, even though we're *In Christ* we are a dysfunctional body. God has given us people as precious treasures. If we don't accept the friendships, mentors, and counselors He provides, our lives will miss much of the richness and depths of joy He has for us.

And so, I too searched saying, "Have you seen the One my heart loves?" I found many on my path. Some said, "No, but I'm seeking Him too. Can we walk together?" Others asked, "Who is He?" and I was able to share my Beloved's love with them.

Scarcely had I passed them when I found the One my heart loves. I held Him and would not let Him go till I had brought Him to my Mother's house, to the chamber of the One who conceived me. **(3:4)**

Even though people are important to our lives, we can't depend too much on them in our relationship with God. Notice the maiden found her

Lover as soon as she left the watchman. This doesn't mean we're not meant to be involved with others. We just can't expect them to fill the longing God put in our soul for Him. That place is His alone.

The maiden's desperation caused her Lover to gladly reveal Himself.[4] His absence was a test to see if she trusted Him completely and would obey instantly, even when He didn't seem to be with her. As these virtues become powerful in her life they will push out all hesitation and complacency.

The Holy Spirit (mother) brought her spirit to life (conceived me). While at rest, the maiden recognized she holds her Lover in her spirit (house), and their new relationship will be Spirit God and spirit man united.

In God's Triune family, He is the Father, Jesus is the Son, and the Holy Spirit represents the mother. This was revealed to me in a vision one day. While in prayer I saw three men dressed in ancient robes. They were standing together having a conversation. When they noticed me watching them, they all waved for me to come over. I felt like a child running to my family. Reflecting on the scene, I knew I had been with my Father, my Brother, and could it be, my Mother? That was weird. But then I realized the Holy Spirit's character is the same as the love and nurturing of a mother as He trains, guides, protects and comforts.

Scripture: *For I am accomplishing a work in your days, a work which you will never believe, though someone should describe it to you.* (Acts 13:41)

For the Kingdom of God does not consist in words, but in power. (I Corinthians 4:20)

... The one who joins himself to the Lord is one spirit with Him. (I Corinthians 6:17)

Prayer: Lord, I've been looking for You. I've tried all I know to do to have more of You in my life. I feel as if You've pulled away so I'll come to the end of myself, and step into You. Thank You for all the people in my life. They're great. But I must step over the line of my flesh life to also live in the Kingdom of the Spirit realm. Please help me learn to be instantly obedient to Your voice.

My Revelation:

Crushing Glory

I adjure you, O daughters of Jerusalem, by the gazelles and by the hinds of the field that you do not arouse or awaken My love until she desires. (3:5)

While the maiden enjoyed spirit to Spirit fellowship with Jesus, the daughters are told to leave her alone. He explained to them what's going to happen. She will be learning to leap and run (hinds) supernaturally in the Spirit Realm.

As she rests in Him, she will know His intimacy more fully. Jesus will become her *Hope of Glory.*

Who is this coming up from the wilderness like a column of smoke, perfumed with myrrh and frankincense made from all the spices of the Merchant? (3:6)

As if watching a play in a theater, the maiden moved off center stage and the scene changed. Suddenly, the daughter's spirit-eyes open. Squinting, as if looking into brilliant sunlight, they see *Someone* approaching from the wilderness (unknown places). *Column of smoke* represents an elusive, supernatural something.

Jesus (The Merchant) creates fragrant powders in His Kingdom (wilderness). When a person passionately pursues the Lord, they will not be denied. The glory of His presence will come. However, His pureness and glory is so powerful, it will press out unholiness, self, or any other hindrances. Glory is weighty, frightening, and powerful, but, oh, so wonderful. One tiny touch of His presence can send us melting to the floor, trembling and shaking foolishly.

I have read when some of the great-saints-of-old experienced God's manifest presence, His glory was so overwhelming they begged Him to leave.

I long to be ready to embrace God's all-encompassing glory. I don't want to be one who says, "No more," as He crushes His fragrance into me.

I didn't know becoming nothing so He could be everything required being pressed flat as a slab by the power of humility. But the crushing process frees Jesus to lay Himself as the cornerstone of our soul. He is the firm foundation that must be established to hold all the other stones representing His character and virtues in our spiritual house.

So when it seems your whole life is being destroyed, don't despair. The Merchant is pressing in to make His scented powder. He won't totally destroy us. His plan is to complete our maturity.

Here's a quote to help us understand. *Because we really want Him, we come to a place where we can look nowhere but to God, and He leaves us hanging there on a thread of faith, clinging to Him and believing Him. If we can do this without wavering, we begin to develop new stronger faith that calls the things that are not as though they were, and we begin to see our mountains removed.*[1]

Those words remind me of the way the Holy Spirit taught me this lesson. He had asked me to give up everything I believed, and to reevaluate what was truth and what was really important. As I yielded to His will He took what I called ministry, and almost everything else I held dear. I felt I'd even lost my identity. Then, in a vision, I saw myself hanging onto the edge of the precipice of a tall cliff. The experience was so real I could feel the gritty dirt of the rock wall under my fingernails. My muscles were in pain, sweat poured down my face. I cried, "Lord, I have nothing left, I'm hanging on by my fingernails here."

His response was, "Let go!"

Shocked as usual by His solution, I realized trust can't even hang on to life. Real trust must release every grain of self-preservation. Letting go, I fell into His pillow-like embrace.

He makes us scented powders for the Merchant by crushing His glory into us, bringing the transformation of who we were created to be.

Scripture: *We have this treasure in earthen vessels, that the surpassing greatness of the power may be of God, and not from ourselves, we are afflicted in every way, but not crushed; perplexed, but not despairing; persecuted, but not forsaken, struck down, but not destroyed, always carrying about in the body the dying of Jesus, that the life of Jesus also may be manifested in our body.*
(II Corinthians 4:7-10)

... for I know the plans I have for you, declares the Lord, plans for welfare and not for calamity, to give you a future and a hope. (Jeremiah 29:11)

Prayer: Lord, I must know truth and what is really important. My mind seems full of confusion and trivia. I truly need the mind of Christ. I don't know if I want to embrace the thought of crushing glory, or run from it. I'll just ask You to prepare me for more. Help me not fear Your out-of-this-world passion.

My Revelation:

Make Way for the King

Look! It is Solomon's carriage, escorted by sixty warriors, the noblest of Israel. The sixty warriors, are wearing the sword, all experienced in battle, each with his sword at his side, and prepared for the terrors of the night. (3:7-8)

In the Spirit, the daughters continue to see a vision of God's Kingdom. They realize they're looking at Solomon's carriage. Royalty is among them.

Imagine long ago the ladies lived in a small peasant village. One day the King's carriage rolled passed, surrounded by His warriors. The grandeur and majesty of the event would be spectacular compared to their common lives. The day the King passed by would be the most memorable experience of their lifetime.

Spiritually, the daughters' eyes have opened. Now, they too can see the Kingdom of God and the magnificence and royalty of their King.

Solomon's carriage is flanked by sixty (completeness[2]) warriors, the very best of the best, skilled with swords (the Word). They are prepared to fight against fear, lies, deception, and anything else keeping His people captive to darkness.

Not only do these warriors fight the enemies of our soul to make room for Jesus's virtues to take root. They're also prepared to fight the terrors of the night for us.

When we face tragedy and upheaval in our lives, the nights can seem like an enemy. The quietness yells confusing and disheartening words until there's no rest. But then, Peace, one of God's virtues, comes as a warrior to do battle so we can sleep in the midst of the storm.

When you lie down you will not be afraid; when you lie down, your sleep will be sweet.

(Proverbs. 3:24)

King Solomon made for Himself a carriage; He made it of cedar from Lebanon. Its pillars He made of silver, the couch is of gold. Its seat was upholstered with purple, its interior lovingly inlaid by the daughters of Jerusalem. (3:9-10)

Through prophetic words, the wide-eyed daughters try to describe the splendor of the carriage. *Cedar of Lebanon* is the symbol of perfect power, majesty, and royalty. *Pillars* are strength and steadfastness. *Silver* describes Jesus's redemption and salvation. *Gold* represents Kingdom glory, and *purple* is royalty.[5] This verse declared, "Here comes the King! He's coming with salvation, power, majesty, royalty, and glory!"

116

Notice, as the virgins matured, and their eyes opened to see in the Spirit realm, they're called daughters of Jerusalem. By watching the bride they awakened spiritually and joined the great progression of change.

Interior lovingly inlaid by the daughters of Jerusalem tells us they also love the King, and they are doing their part in helping to prepare the way for His Kingdom.

Scripture: *She will be led to the King in embroidered work. The virgins, her companions who follow her, will be brought to thee ... and they will enter into the King's palace.* (Psalm 45:14)

We all, as His church, have the power to hasten the day of His return. (II Peter 3:12)

Prayer: Lord, we have prayed for Your Kingdom to come but we had no idea what we were really asking. Open our spirit-eyes to recognize Your Kingdom has come. You've already provided everything for us with Your protection, provision, and even sleep. Amazing. You had Solomon tell us all about Your wonders so long ago, yet we're still struggling to know Your love. I repent. You have also revealed the whole human race is bound together as Your bride. And as we

117

chase after You, others will be free to come to You too. Help me be quick to help them win their race.

My Revelation:

The Wedding

Go forth, O daughters of Zion, and behold King Solomon, with the crown with which His mother has crowned Him on the day of His wedding, and on the day of the gladness of His heart. (3:11)

This verse reveals more advancement for the daughters. They have become daughters of Zion, God's Kingdom. As each of us mature in the Lord personally, we're also spiritually attached by the Holy Spirit to one another. As we move forward with God, others are also drawn ahead.

The maiden cried out to the daughters of Zion, "Come and see the beauty of our Bridegroom King. We were right. There *is* more for us to know about Jesus. The Holy Spirit is the one drawing, calling, and wooing us to know God more fully. You *will not* be disappointed."

Mother (Holy Spirit) has everything ready for the wedding. The crown of the Prince of peace and King of kings is on His head in ceremonial dress for the wedding. Jesus's heart is full as He's united with His bride in marriage. She has given all she is to Him, just as He rendered all for her. This is *Union with*

God! Complete union, which is none of me and all of God.[6]

But, let's pause and reflect on the words *His gladness of heart.* Jesus left the glory of heaven to come to earth as a human to give His life so He could have His bride. He interceded on her behalf for centuries, waiting for the day she would be His. He watched and loved her while she often ignored Him. He waited as she pursued other lovers because self was her God. But the Father promised one day Jesus would have His bride. His heart rejoices because the day has finally come. The Holy Spirit has completed His work. The bride has made herself ready.

Scripture: *Let us rejoice and be glad and give the glory to Him for the marriage of the Lamb has come and His bride has made herself ready.* (Revelation 19:7)

I will betroth you to Me forever... (Hosea 2:19)

Prayer: I've never considered a wedding with You, Lord, except maybe in the after-life. But You want us to be wed spirit to Spirit now. Yes Lord. I trust You, and choose to be a bride who has made herself ready. I love being loved by You.

The Honeymoon

While seeking the Lord, I kept a journal. Quietly waiting before Him, I wrote down whatever I thought God said. My mind filled with adoring words, and I questioned where all the delightful expressions of love were coming from. The thoughts couldn't have been my own because I wasn't very affectionate toward anyone, especially myself. But, in the privacy of my journal I wrote words too lovely for me to believe.

Later, while reading Song of Solomon, I realized the phrases in the verses sounded the same as the words I'd secretly written in my journal. The thoughts I'd jotted down and given no credibility, *were* God speaking to me.

He really does want us to hear His divine words of love for us. In fact, they are ringing continually through the universe in the hope ears will be open to hear their truth. They are forever repeating, waiting for us to receive them, when we finally have ears to hear. He is saying,

How fair you are, My love; how beautiful you are! Your eyes behind your veil are doves. (4:1)

The couple entered a new relationship. Marriage. Remember my description of the spiral staircase up the center of my soul house. At this point in our maturity, the maiden and I stood at the bottom of the stairs. The construction was complete, the scaffolding gone.

The little bride cautiously climbed the stairs of her finished soul house. She found herself at the door of the King's chambers. She entered and stood before Him. Though trembling, she dropped her gown as her last hope of reserve, becoming naked before Him. Though completely vulnerable on their wedding night, she wouldn't hold anything back from her King and Lover. He looked at her with heaven's love and pleasure, then reached for His purple robe of righteousness and wrapped her in its warmth as they came together.

The maiden has found acceptance and love. She wants to stay in His purity and holy bliss forever.

Now, in the same way we heard romantic expressions during their courtship, we're allowed to hear love's passion in the privacy of the newlywed's bridal chamber. Imagine the intimacy of this place. The bride has come to Him completely vulnerable. He welcomed her into His arms. It's a passionate embrace of pleasure and happiness.

The King, ever so gently began to admire his bride's features. The joy He feels is like a man unwrapping the most wonderful gift he could ever receive, and it is all His (My love).

There's great satisfaction when a groom finally has the woman he loves all to himself.

Jesus experiences the same feelings with His bride, only magnified beyond explanation. He has waited through time for her to finally be His.

Lovemaking begins as He studies her beautiful face. He describes His own reflection in her pure (doves) eyes as fair, meaning *without spot or wrinkle.* (Ephesians 5:27)

Veil here doesn't mean separation as it did before. Now the word describes a virtue. She is trustworthy, protecting the secrets He reveals to her. Some things aren't meant to be shared of this holy union. Virtues, discernment, and holy wisdom help her perceive with spiritual insight. The veil protects what her pure spirit-eyes are allowed to behold.[1]

Your hair is like a flock of ewe descending from Mount Gilead (4:1)

In the couple's private marriage chamber, the bride lets her hair fall over her shoulders showing love's submission. She is yielded and uninhibited by old concerns. There's no fear in letting Him see who she really is because she knows she can trust Him.

We would say she is free to let her hair down, or be her real self.

Her teeth are like a flock of newly shorn sheep, like ewes coming up from the water after they have been washed. Each has its twin; not one is barren among them. **(4:2)**

These are such strange words to describe a bride, but teeth represent understanding, memory, and imagination.[5] These virtues are now her character as a mature sheep (female ewe). She is also abundantly fruitful, twice blessed (twins). As she reflects Jesus, those she nurtures with wisdom reflect her. She can freely say *Follow me as I follow Christ.* (II Thessalonians 3:9) *as she is bringing many sons to glory.* (Hebrews 2:10)

Your lips are like a scarlet thread, and your speech is sweet. **(4:3)**

The Beloved is pleased with the kisses of her lips. Purity came through the pressure and tests that taught her to yield to the challenges required to develop sweet, loving voice tones in her words.

When God draws close, His holiness rests on us. This holy weightiness can bring awareness of the vileness of words. Not the language of a sinner, but the impure words of a saint.

124

For me, this happened, fortunately, over a week I was able to be alone with the Lord. As I spent time with Him, His presence manifested. Holiness filled my house until I was overcome with the abomination of my humanness.

I had spoken very little. The simple word *hello* to a wrong number on the phone overwhelmed me with an awareness of my filthiness.

I *knew* how to guard my tongue, and I longed for a pure heart, knowing it's out of the heart the mouth speaks, (Matthew 12:34) but this was something different.

Holy God was revealing to me the unholiness of the human race. I also knew what it meant to be "undone." The unsettling disruption was so shaking, I wondered if what I was experiencing could be some sort of emotional breakdown.

Finally, I realized this was something new the Spirit had for me because I'd shut away to be with Him. I didn't like it.

During the unnatural pressure of the Holy Spirit taking more ownership of my life, I understood what Isaiah experienced when he encountered the Living God in His holiness.

I cried out as Isaiah did, "Forgive me Lord; *I am a man of unclean lips.*" (Isaiah 6:5)

In that time, God revealed how far off my goodness was compared to His holiness. What a reality check. The truth is, no matter how hard I try, I'll always be a sinner saved by God's grace. So, in those pressured moments, I came to know God in a new way; by His name *Grace.*

The revelation brought me lower than ever, and in the humbling place, judgment died. A sinner like me must never judge anyone.

In knowing grace, the bride's speech is grace-filled. Her voice brings love, authority, wisdom, and knowledge. When she speaks, desperate people listen and find hope. The Bridegroom is pleased her testimony (scarlet thread) is delightfully tasteful (sweet) to humanity.

The bride had respect for the new sound of her voice. Seeing the authority it carried and recognizing the awesome privilege of sharing God's message of love, she asked for a holy guard to be placed over her anointed lips so words would be pure and powerful as she declared His truth.

Scripture: ... *As a bridegroom rejoices over his bride so will your God rejoice over you.* (Isaiah 62:5)

Let the beauty of the Lord our God be upon us ... (Psalm 90:17)

126

Prayer: Lord, now I realize these scriptures are Your personal love letters to me. You sound like You're delighted with everything about me. I've got to quit being so hard on myself. Thank You, for revealing Your love and passion for me as Your bride today. I realize I don't need to wait until I die to enjoy Your loving presence. Thanks Lord, for Your grace. I would be happy to spend my life learning to know that one characteristic of Your names. Grace truly is amazing.

My Revelation:

The Honeymoon Continues

Jesus is never in a rush as He lavishes love and affection on His bride. We are the ones who hurry off to do life. He is continually expressing His love for us.

Your temples behind your veil are like the halves of a pomegranate (4:3)

Not only is the Groom enjoying her body, but He's also pleased with her mind (temples). The Holy Spirit, as her veil, has fine-tuned her to understand Kingdom ways.

Let this mind be in you which is also in Jesus Christ. (Philippians 2:5)

A pomegranate is an unusual fruit. When I opened one for the first time, it was full of small red seeds. I wondered about their purpose. I'd heard the juice was good for our health. Perhaps the deep ruby color had been used for dye.

In the same way I started thinking about the possibilities of the seeds, the Holy Spirit began to open (halves) the Word to me in new ways. When I read the Bible, it seemed as if someone threw all the words into the air, and they were swirling around suspended above my head. When a few words finally landed, I was astounded by the new insight. It was as if I'd never read the Word before, as God revealed His grace and love throughout His Holy Scriptures.

Trying to lay aside everything I previously understood, I opened my heart to receive the Holy Spirit's new revelation. If someone asked my opinion on a subject, my answer became, "I know nothing, I'm undone." But somehow those words felt like they were a declaration of progress. Peace came by realizing whatever I learned in the future would be from heart-to-heart communion with the Holy Spirit. My mind (temples) was covered with the Holy Spirit's presence (veil) to help me know truth.

Be renewed in the spirit of your mind. (Ephesians 4:23)

We have the mind of Christ. (I Corinthians 2:16)

Love the Lord with all of your mind. (Matthew 22:37)

Your neck is like the tower of David, (4:4)

In the intimacy of love, the Bridegroom admired her neck. He enjoyed the way it turned as He moved, always following without question. In total abandonment, she declared, *Thy will be done.* By surrendering her will (the opposite of stiff-necked) to

His, she could be described as David was. *A man after God's own heart.* (Acts 13:22)

Built up with bulwarks, a thousand shields hang upon it, All of them shields of warriors. (4:4)

A bulwark is a wall of defense. The victories fought for and won in prayer and faith hang as trophies (thousand shields) in the completed tower (bulwarks).[1]

Sometimes, while praying about a situation, I'm reminded of another problem in the past, and remember the way God brought His victory. His answers from other battles in prayer hang on the wall of my tower (mind and soul) to remind me He did it before, so He can do it again. Then my faith takes hold of the previous victory, and I can believe for another miracle. I know God is able and willing because of His faithfulness in the past.

When God answers prayer, and a loved-one is healed of cancer, no one can tell me God doesn't heal sickness. Watching God restore a marriage everyone said was too far gone explodes faith in me to believe He will do it again. Seeing a prodigal come home and find wholeness and health proves God's grace and mercy, and confirms He continues to restore lives. Holding a baby in my arms people declared would never be born reminds me to grab hold of God's promise that His handmaidens will have their children. These testimonies are trophies hanging on the walls of our souls.

Your two breasts are like two fawns, like twin fawns of a gazelle that browse among the lilies. **(4:5)**

In the Kingdom realm breasts represent faith and love. The progression of love's passion in the bridal chamber finds the Bridegroom enjoying the intimacy of His bride's breasts. God is just as delighted with His bride's maturing faith and love as a human bridegroom finds pleasure in his bride's physical bosoms. Both spiritual and natural breasts grow as twins. Love for God causes faith to grow just as faith in Him releases more love.

Her young breasts are developing quickly (gazelle) because they feed on God's purity (lilies).

Faith and love are always in partnership.

... the only thing that counts is faith expressing itself through love. (Galatians 5:6)

The goal of this command is love, which comes from a pure heart and faith. (I Timothy 1:5)

... put on the breastplate of faith and love. (I Thessalonians 5:8)

Until the day breaks and the shadows flee away, I will get Me to the mountains of myrrh and to the hill of frankincense. **(4:6)**

Right in the middle of Solomon's dialog about Jesus's pleasure with His bride, He stopped. Pausing, he looked away from the revelation of her beauty. A new scene unfolded before his eyes. Prophetically, he described what was before him.

Jesus goes to Calvary.

Solomon explained a great price would be paid for the King to have His perfect bride. He shared the salvation message.

Daybreak is the day when salvation would come to bring her perfection. *Shadows flee* represents Jesus going to the cross to suffer *(mountain of myrrh)* and die *(hill of Frankincense or Golgotha).*

Solomon prophetically looked ahead through time and saw Jesus declare His unconditional love for His perfected radiant bride. He watched as our Savior went to the cross and paid the price for redemption with His blood.

You are altogether beautiful, My darling; there is no flaw in you. **(4:7)**

Then he turned back to look at the bride. The work was complete. Jesus, the perfect sacrifice bought her redemption. She is flawless.

Scripture: *... that He might present to Himself the Church in all of her glory, having no spot or wrinkle or any such thing; but that she should be holy and blameless.* (Ephesians 5:27)

Prayer: Lord, Thank You, for redemption, and Your sacrifice allowing me to be Your perfect bride. When Solomon prophetically saw You go to the cross for us, he also saw me as beautiful and flawless. I choose today to live the perfect life You provided for me. I don't know how, but I invite You, Holy Spirit, to remind me who I really am. Help me brush off all other voices so I can believe You. Open my spirit-ears and eyes to know the reality of Your Kingdom. Thank You, for continuing to mature my faith and love. Thanks for the trophies in my soul that remind me of Your faithfulness.

My Revelation:

The High Call

Come with Me from Lebanon, My Bride, may you come with Me from Lebanon, come; you will be crowned from the top of Amana, from the peak of Shenir and Hermon, **(4:8)**

Jesus urged His bride to come from Lebanon (pure) three times in this verse. When the Holy Spirit needs to tell me the same thing a third time, the words shake my spirit to its core. I want what He wants, but sometimes the changes are so great, and my understanding so small, I feel the need to be sure it's really the Holy Spirit speaking. When He uses the same words three times, I tremble knowing there's no time to waste. I don't pause and think the decision over anymore, but repent for my delay and quickly obey.

This verse is describing Jesus's plans for after their honeymoon. The Bridegroom wants His bride to come *from* Lebanon. Come from purity's place to be crowned His Queen.

Prophetically, Amana means *truth,* Shenir is *soft armor,* and Herman refers to the destruction caused by Jesus's victory on the cross.[4] Taking the simplicity of each name, this verse is saying, *Come from purity, My wife, come from purity and be My Queen (crown)*

135

in the Kingdom of God (top) where truth (Amana)
reigns. Receive My power, and the armor of God for
battle (Shenir). From the heights I will show you
victory (Herman). Come and be a Kingdom warrior.

Earlier, the Beloved asked His bride to follow
Him. Their marriage has brought matured trust.
Unity made her His confidant. For the first time, the
Bridegroom gives His wife the full itinerary of His
plans.

I will do nothing without telling my prophets.
(Amos 3:7)

Knowing Kingdom reality makes it possible to see
from God's perspective. To learn spiritual warfare
from His realm requires the clear view which comes
from our position with Jesus in His Throne room.
From that high place, it's much easier to recognize
the deception of the enemy.

This is the first time the Bridegroom used the
phrase *My Bride*. The verse also reveals a key to our
Kingdom life. God always invites us to join Him in
what's ahead. In this case, He is calling her to
Oneness. We know they've already been married
awhile. However, we're also aware, just because two
people get married it doesn't really make them one.
This happens as they share their lives together and
learn to live in unity.

The King also called her His Queen. His Bride is
at His side on His Throne in the Kingdom of God.

Scripture: ... *At His right hand stands the queen clothed in the gold of Ophir.* (Psalm 45:9)

... I will set him securely on high, because he has known My name. (Psalm 91:14)

He will dwell on the heights; His refuge will be the impregnable rock ... (Isaiah 33:16)

Your eyes will see the King in His beauty; They will behold a far-distant land. (Isaiah 33:17)

God raised us up with Him, and seated us with Him in the heavenly places, in Christ Jesus. (Ephesians 2:6)

He who overcomes, I will grant to sit down with Me on My throne, as I also overcame and sat down with My Father on His throne. (Revelation 3:21)

Prayer: Lord, You are preparing me for the high call of being Jesus's Queen. Help me grasp this concept. I'm still trying to understand being married to Jesus. This just keeps getting bigger. You mean I'm also meant to reign with You, and sit beside You in Your Spirit realm? I repent of taking what the Word says too lightly.

Please, transform my mind so I can understand all You have for me. I defiantly understand what feeling *undone* is.

My Revelation:

The Warrior Bride

From the den of lions from the mountains of leopards. (4:8)

Satan, the enemy of our soul, is being described here. Just as heaven's angels are real and present in the world around us, our hellish enemy has his servants. The Word calls them principalities and powers of the air, or demons. Some people insist our thoughts of them are fantasy. I promise you they are not. These spirits hope to keep us in the dark about their existence so they can take advantage of our ignorance, and their reality will remain a secret. They use their evil ways to block us so we won't find God's love. True life can be sucked out of us when temptations bring addictions, wrong attitudes cause hatred, and lust steals our resources, and perhaps, even our soul. Such things hinder our ability to experience the fullness of the life God wants us to enjoy. They sidetrack us from the glorious destiny He chose for our lives.

The evil ones make their camp (den) in the high places at the borders of the Kingdom of God. *Lions* are a symbol of the enemy as a roaring foe seeking whom he can devour. He is strong, and persevering, but bitter and full of hatred toward God and man.

Leopards represent the enemy as a fierce, swift foe, enraged against mankind. In Revelation 13:2 the leopard is used as a symbol of the Antichrist.[1]

As the Lord called His Bride to supernatural heights, He forewarned her of the new trials she would face. She'll battle in territory never before taken for the Kingdom of God. These skirmishes sound too overwhelming. Surely we're not meant to fight them.

Just as a princess is trained to represent the throne, the Holy Spirit prepared the Bride to live a life of divine royalty as Jesus's Warrior Bride. She has developed spirit-ears to can hear thing not even spoken. The Holy Spirit quickly helped her discern what was in another's heart. She encouraged each soul with life-giving words that flowed from lips declaring the truth of God's love for them. With supernatural vision, she can see God's great Host standing close ready to fight every battle with her.

The Holy Spirit gave her instructions on how to lighten her load, and simplify her life even more than in the past. He taught her to be strong in warfare, swift in movement, and sure-footed as a hind (meaning her spirit will easily leap into the Spirit realm just as her Lover does).

Trained with the strict discipline of a fine-tuned jungle fighter, she knows the strategies her enemy employs, and she has the ability needed for victory.

As she enters where evil dominates, she's fully prepared to defeat her foe and seize the unconquered territories of the opposing spirit realm.

Earthlings never enter here. Dark forces have dominion in these high places, which have been guarded by powerful demonic strongholds throughout history. Only a very few, covered in Jesus's blood and the power of humility, have passed through this ominous place.

She could not, and will not, be the one to fight this battle. The Holy Spirit will supernaturally fight through her.

At this very hard place of facing the enemy of God toe to toe, it helps to remember Satan was created by God. Our Father Deliverer uses the satanic strongholds for a purpose. They test to see if the Bride is worthy to enter. Of course, all worthiness comes from dying to self, abiding in Christ, and willingly saying, "Yes Lord."

As the Bride moves into the fullness of the Kingdom of God, Satan will use every weapon in his arsenal to desperately keep his ground. Oppressive spirits will try to bring discouragement, confusion, and exhaustion, which can be overwhelming. Especially if the enemy can keep what he's doing a secret.

But the Bride recognized the opposition's warfare. She stayed humble and free from fear by keeping her eyes on Jesus, and her ears tuned to the Holy Spirit. Soon she will receive her crown.

After the Bride engaged the hellish beasts face to face, she was astonished to find the skirmishes were less difficult than expected. Jesus's blinding light of glory shined through her as she stood before those in darkness. The Hosts of Heaven was at her side with their flashing swords drawn. Light fought her war.

When we battle alongside Jesus, who is Light, through the dark lines of defense in these high places, Satan *will* lose.[1] As the winners of this battle, we will dwell in the very places the defeated one lived.

He prepares a table before me in the presence of my enemies. (Psalm 23:5)

However, the antagonist's real work is primarily to devour those who don't fight the good fight of faith (I Timothy 6:12) and finish the race. So don't give up.

By living from heaven's perspective in the high places, the Bride understands how demonic forces bind people, and she has the keys to set them free. Her success causes many demons to lose their homes. They scatter like bugs do when you turn over a rock. Or the squirmy ghouls might come out roaring, or squealing like pigs, as they run to find a new hiding place.

After every battle, she must cleanse herself from the stench of hell's pollution by declaring the blood of

Jesus over her life. Just using those words washes her in purity again. As she rejoices in winning victories she will declare, *I will fear no evil; for You are with me.* (Psalm 23:4)

Scripture: *For our struggle is not against flesh and blood, but against the rulers, against the powers, against the world forces of this darkness, against the spiritual forces of wickedness in the heavenly places.* (Ephesians 6:12)

I have fought the good fight, I have finished the race, I have kept the faith. (II Timothy 4:7)

... the kingdom of heaven suffers violence, and violent men take it by force. (Matthew 11:12)

... put on the armor of light. (Romans 13:12)

Prayer: Lord, by faith I confess I am Your warrior bride. Prepare me to face every battle You have for me to fight. Help me have the discernment to recognize the skirmishes You want me to engage. Free me to move quickly as Your brave warrior who is full of light, righteousness, truth, and love. Help my spirit man recognize the heavenly host You have provided to help me, so I can accomplish much more than I could ever do alone.

My Revelation:

Ravished Heart

You have ravished My heart, My sister, My spouse; you have stolen My heart with one glance of your eyes, **(4:9)**

The Bride went to the borders where the enemy dwelled, and fought until new gates opened, making the way for her to get to her Lover.

The Bridegroom's words of love drew her to Himself right through a minefield of evil. He is thrilled to see how splendidly she uses her authority.

I find this verse staggering. God, who created the universe, said, and continues to say to us, His heart is *ravished*. The meaning of the word is: *captivated, enraptured, transported with pleasure, to seize and carry away by violence.* (Webster) I should take a whole day to meditate on this one word allowing the Holy Spirit to teach me how absolutely in love with me He really is.

It's hard to fathom our God, who is love, being torn up with excitement as He watches His Bride. His emotions must be off the charts by human comparison. The glory of our Savior's excitement and passion over her success is beyond comprehension.

I can almost see Him standing in the courts of heaven shouting, "Look at my champion Bride who is powerfully fighting to be fully united with Me. She is Mine. Mine. She loves Me with all of her heart, soul, strength, and mind. (Matthew 22:37)

But, isn't it curious as He shared His passion for His Bride He also called her sister? Our society would never think a sister would be a more intimate description than wife.

Prophetically, the word reveals she has received a new bloodline that allows her to share in the full inheritance of their Father.

Marriage represents union until death on earth, but the brother-sister bloodline is forever.[1]

The Bride has received His holy blood transfusion. Now, divine blood flows through her veins. She has become royalty with King Jesus.

Scriptures: ... *eyes have not seen and ear has not heard ... or entered the heart of man all that God has prepared for those who love Him.* (I Corinthians 2:9)

... you are a ... royal priesthood ... God's own possession ... (I Peter 2:9)

Prayer: Your heart is ravished for me Lord? What does that even look like? You seem to want us so passionately, yet You wait for us to come to You. I choose today to fight the good fight of faith, (II Timothy 4:7) and go through the doors waiting for me to enter to be with You. Holy Spirit, don't give up on me. Continue to push me into God's best, which is His ravished heart of love.

My Revelation:

The King's Delight

with one jewel of your necklace. (4:9)

As the Bride won victories in her battles, her reward was her Lover's heart. Now, He is free to passionately express His affection for her. The King is satisfied in every way with the woman (no longer a maiden) He married. He describes His Queen. One glance of her eyes ravished His heart because they reflect the pureness of a perfect soul. She's become the completion of all He wanted when He said, *Be perfect as I am perfect.* (Matthew 5:48)

In verse 1:9 the Bride was described as having a string of jewels around her neck, which represented the books of the Bible. In this verse she is wearing one jewel. Jesus, the Word, now adorns her neck.

In the beginning was the Word, and the Word was with God and the Word was God. (John 1:1)

How fair are your breasts, My sister spouse! Your breasts are fairer than wine and the fragrance of your oils than all kinds of spices. **(4:10)**

The Bridegroom expressed His delight as He said, "Your faith and love (breasts) are without flaw, My wife of royal blood, My Queen Bride (spouse). More perfect than any other delights (wine). The presence (fragrance) and anointing (oil) of the Holy Spirit in you are a pure reflection of My Kingdom."

Your lips, My Spouse, drip like a honeycomb: honey and milk are under your tongue (4:11)

As the King described the beauty of her lips, I imagine He paused to reflect on the fact she finally belongs to Him. There's a sound of glorious satisfaction in His voice as He spoke the words, "My Spouse." Oh, if only each of us would hear these words from Jesus as He declares His delight with us.

His Bride speaks sweet, life-giving words bring refreshment (honey). *How sweet are Thy words to my taste! Yes, sweeter than honey to my mouth.* (Psalm 119:103)

and the smell of your garments is like the smell of Lebanon. (4:11)

This would be a wonderful place to study the preparation Esther experienced before she was presented to her King. There comes a time in all of us when the spiritual readiness required to be Jesus's Queen is complete. Scripture says, *He who has begun a good work will be faithful to complete it.* (Philippians 1:6) We can trust God to establish His plan for our life.

There's an expression called *soaking* today, meaning resting and receiving the Holy Spirit's manifest presence until we're saturated with His glory.

The Bride has been *In Him* and is clothed with purity. The fragrance of the Kingdom of God owns her. This is similar to when we sit by a campfire, or cook in the kitchen, and carry the aroma of our environment.

Her appearance, manner of speech, yes, even her slightest gestures are permeated with the perfume of His dwelling (cedar), and the sweet-scent of heaven (Mount Lebanon's purity).[1]

One of the fragrances of her spiritual perfume is peace. The Bride has died to self-preservation, worry, and doubt. The presence of peace shows in her nerves, words, and hand movements.

Peace is foreign to the world. When people see its presence in someone's life, they're in awe. Peace is a person. His name is Jesus.

Scripture: ... *The Lord will bless His people with peace.* (Psalm 29:11)

The humble will inherit the land and will delight themselves in an abundance of peace. (Psalm 37:11)

Those who love Your law have great peace, and nothing causes them to stumble. (Psalm 119:165)

... of His government of peace there will be no end to the increase. (Isaiah 9:7)

For we are the fragrance of Christ to God among those who are being saved and those who are perishing. (II Corinthians 2:15)

Prayer: Lord, I delight in You. I want to soak in Your fragrance until I smell of Your loveliness. I ask for Your peace-filled countenance in my actions and words. Cleanse me of all worries and frustration. I want to reflect Your character by living a life of peace. Thank You, that Your love is building my faith to believe all these things are possible.

My Revelation:

The Garden

A garden shut up, My sister, My Bride; a rock garden locked, a spring sealed shut. Your plants are an orchard of pomegranates with choice fruits, henna with nard plants, spikenard and saffron: calamus and cinnamon, with every kind of incense tree, with myrrh and aloes and all the finest spices. **(4:12-14)**

These words reveal something wonderfully mystical. I'll share my experience to explain. I was teaching a group of ladies the idea of us being God's garden. When finished, I felt I should pray for each person. Amazingly, as I touched the first woman I saw a garden. I knew the Holy Spirit was showing me the garden of her soul, so I describe it to her in detail.

Moving from one person to another, I saw each soul's garden. They were all uniquely different. One of the unusual gardens was in a deep hole. Rock walls were covered with blooming plants. A woman said, "I've seen a garden like that. They turned a rock quarry into a beautiful flower garden."

Another soul revealed an English garden full of colorful flowers. The next garden was a totally green area with many varieties of leafy foliage. Still another had a little cottage in the middle and the lady stood in the door welcoming guests.

I couldn't get over how quickly the vision's changed as I moved from one lady to another. God was confirming my teaching by allowing me to see His unconventional land in His people. Surely, I was more in awe of the experience than anyone else.

This was one of those times God opened my spirit-eyes to see unseen things. I didn't even know the name of many of the unique flowers I saw.

A garden (soul) is where Jesus feels at home. His fellowship with Adam and Eve in the garden ended because of disobedience. But now, sin's price has been paid, and He enjoys having fellowship within us.

The Holy Spirit was a gentle gardener with His Bride as He pulled out bitter roots, and cursed generational roots from her soul. He restored all the inner ground given to Him by creating a garden where love and all good things were planted. Now she is an orchard of mature fruit in abundance (pomegranates).

Each plant mentioned in this verse represents the Fruit of the Spirit. The Holy Spirit has completed His labors. A harvest of love, joy, peace, patience, kindness, goodness, faithfulness, and self-control are blooming and bearing fruit in full maturity. (Galatians 5:22-23)

God does wonderful things as He works in the garden of our soul. We often don't notice changes taking place as the fruit of the Spirit matures. But then one day, something happens and there's a realization you have a new attitude and healthy emotions.

This happened for me at the lake. One beautiful summer day, my husband and I headed out to ride our wave runners. Before leaving, he said the water was low so we should stay away from the shallow areas. I agreed and off we went. As we zoomed across the water he turned into the exact place he told me to avoid. I thought ... well, you can guess what I thought. But I followed, and soon I was dragging on the bottom of a sandbar. The rocky bottom was clearly visible about two feet down, but as I started to step off and break myself free, an unnatural fear of snakes held me captive. I didn't see anything but clean pebbles underneath, but I felt frozen on my boat. When Jim saw I was stuck, he yelled back, "Just get off and push yourself into deeper water." Ready to put my foot in, I realized I was upset. Suddenly, I heard words from somewhere outside my mind saying, "Here is where you chew him up one side and down the other."

That's right, I thought. Ready to tell him off, I paused in wonder. There wasn't any anger in my heart. I only felt soft gentleness toward him. What a surprising change.

As I turned my attention back to fixing the situation, my sweet man splashed over, pushed me free, and saved the day. Back on the dock he looked ready for his tongue-lashing. Instead, I gave him a big hug while thanking him for being my hero. We were both pleased with the change in my heart.

God allowed the experience to show me the work He had done in my heart through my desire to have His attitudes. Normally, I wouldn't have feared snakes in the water. Nor would we have gone to the unusable area. The enemy saw an opportunity to bring discord, but my heart didn't have anything in it to use. Amazing.

This is what God can do in our soul garden. Create a brand new heart of love by removing anger and the need for revenge.

Scripture: *Create in me a clean heart, O God, and renew a steadfast spirit within me.* (Psalm 51:10)

This is how my Father is glorified, that you bear much fruit and so prove to be My disciples. (John 15:8)

Prayer: Thank You, Lord, for giving us everything we need. You provide living water to mature

heavenly fruit in us so we can do what's right. Please
pull all unhealthy, generational roots and bitter
roots out of my soul. Replace them with a perfect
fruit garden You will enjoy.

My Revelation:

Fountains Flowing

*You are a garden fountain, a well of flowing
water streaming down from Lebanon.* **(4:15)**

In these words the Bridegroom explained to the
Bride He is in the center of her soul. He has released
His Living Water so it flows through her continually.
She is now an aqueduct for the Kingdom of God to
pour into her city, nation, and the world.

For some time, my dreams were very soggy.
Water flowed through the caverns of my soul. Water
fell from the top of a high mountain and surrounded
my house. There was no way to contain it.
Sometimes it seeped through the foundations, or ran
down the walls and ruined the paint. It soaked the
wood floors, or covered the tile. Water was
everywhere.

In those dreams, I was always trying to figure out
what to do about my problems, just as I would if my
natural house was flooding. At times, the repairman
(Holy Spirit) would come in and tell me the water
wasn't a concern. He said to just let it flow.

There were continuous dreams of water in my
living room. Each time it was worse. Finally, I
dreamed workers came to my home and said the

problem was repaired. However, when I walked into the main room I found they fixed the trouble by putting a huge fountain right in the center. It filled the whole space. Water gushed over several graduated tiers, across the floor, and out the door. Frustrated, I thought surely that wasn't the best fix.

As I prayed to understand, the Holy Spirit explained the dream. I was thrilled. The River of Life had begun to flow freely through my life. I am, as we all are, being prepared to be the aqueduct for Living Water to flow through my city and nation.

Scriptures: Jesus said: ... *I am the Alpha and Omega, the beginning and the end. I will give to the one who thirsts from the spring of the water of life without cost.* (Revelation 21:6)

For with Thee is the fountain of life ... (Psalm 36:9)

For I am accomplishing a work in your days, a work which you will never believe, though someone should describe it to you. (Acts 13:41)

Prayer: Lord, Thank You I don't need to take my dreams literally. Help me learn the dreams are You revealing things to me as I sleep. I've already learned if I dream about houses, it's about my soul, and water is the flow of Your Spirit. Help me remember to write my dreams down so I can pray for understanding. Thank You for having more plans for me than I can ever imagine.

My Revelation:

Trinity Love

The honeymoon garden is complete. The River of Life flows freely through the Bride. Once before, she thought herself to be fully mature, but then she became His warrior bride. Perhaps there is even more for her. God's supernatural ways have far surpassed her understanding.

The gift of humility made her aware of being blind to her own sinfulness and imperfections. So again, she freely opened herself to whatever God had for her. She prayed Psalms 139:23, *Search me, Oh God, and know my heart and see if there is any wicked ways in me.* Or she said:

Arise, north wind, and come, south wind; blow through my garden and let its spices flow out. (4:16)

Concerned there could still be more layers of self, she wants to be sure purity, as her most powerful weapon, is perfected so she'll be safe from danger when she goes to the high places where the flesh-eating devourers camp. Her declaration in this verse is, "I want to die a deeper death."

The first time I heard those words in a song I was stunned. How can someone die more deeply? It seemed to me dead is dead. The words haunted me with possibilities. Could people die to themselves even more than giving everything?

Then I learned after a person is dead, their cells are still alive for a while. Fingernails and hair continue to grow. Therefore, even when I think I've completely died to my flesh, there may still be cells of impurity. Yes, I must die a deeper death so I can live in the high places with Jesus.

She said, "Send the cold, bitter north winds, or warm, gentle south winds. Whatever gale or breeze is needed for Your perfect plan to be fulfilled, I *trust* You."

Spiritual maturity made it possible for her to pray, "Thy will be done," and really mean it because she had no personal agenda. Life no longer needed to be planned and predictable. Maturity welcomes the *unknown*.

The Holy Spirit came as the north wind revealing her nakedness. This takes place in the Spirit realm, but it feels as if being exposed in the natural. It's embarrassing for someone to see our warts and bulges. This is even truer as the Holy Spirit looks for every spiritual blemish and flaw in our soul and spirit. This high calling wind leaves no room to be uncomfortably naked before God, the way Adam and Eve were when they hide in shame. (Genesis 3:8)

I want to be so free of myself I can come naked before Jesus in absolute abandonment. Then, as He looks at my purity, I'll know the innocence of Adam and Eve before their fall. I'll understand the light of the glory that surrounded them as clothing. The Bride is meant to be clothed in the glory of God, wearing His royal robe of Righteousness.

The pure in heart sees everything pure. (Psalm 18:26)

The pure in heart will see God. (Matthew 5:8)

As the winds purge and purify, faith's maturity becomes more than a fruit of the Spirit, or even the *gift of faith.* Faith is one of God's names. It has substance as firm as a foundation of stone.

By fixing her eyes on Jesus during the hard times (winds), her heart was made perfectly faith-filled.

All the trials and training freed her to live in the Holy Spirit's love. He is the third person in her love triangle. God has, in all purity, given us His Trinity of love. There are three lovers who honor each other. As pursuing lovers, the love of the Holy Spirit draws the Bride to Jesus, the loving Bridegroom, who then delights in bringing her to His Father, who is Love. (I John 4:8)

By revelation, the Holy Spirit showed me the love I was experiencing with God was so big it was more like having three lovers in a passionate romance. I saw a short vision of the Trinity falling over each other in their delightful pursuit of me, and I thought, *Oh, brother, Lord, am I supposed to tell people this?* God is so good. He gave me this old prayer to confirm that someone else understood what I'd been shown.

Prayer:
A PRAYER OF THE ANCIENT CELTS

In the fellowship of the gracious Father of glory, in the fellowship of the Spirit of powerful aid, I am lying down tonight with God. And God tonight will lie down with me. I will not lie down tonight with sin, nor shall sin or sin's shadow lie down with me.

I am lying down tonight with the Holy Spirit, and the Holy Spirit this night will lie down with me. I will lie down this night with the Three of my love, and the Three of my love will lie down with me.
Unknown

Scripture: Jesus said, *I will ask the Father, and He will give you another Helper, that He may be with you forever: that is the Spirit of truth ...* (John 14:16-17)

Jesus said, *I and the Father are one.* (John 10:30)

The Winds

The Holy Spirit's work is finished. He decorated
His home within the Bride's soul with His choice of
beautiful things. She's filled with every good and
perfect gift, (James 1:17) ready to accomplish His
purposes. She says,

***Blow into my garden so that its fragrance may
spread abroad. Let my Lover come into His
garden and taste its choice fruits.*** **(4:16)**

Enjoying newfound freedom and seeing glimpses
of the Glory Realm, she asked the Holy Spirit to
carry (blow) her into the fullness of His Kingdom
(abroad). She has no hesitation in going forth now.
In fact, she asked to proceed.

He said *You shall be holy for I am holy.* (I Peter
1:16) However, she never dreamed of being holy in
this lifetime. She thought holiness wouldn't be
possible until she received her glorified body in
heaven.

With purity's completion, the Bride invited her
Bridegroom home for supper. She wanted Him to
enjoy the food He prepared in her by planting His
Tree of Life, and the *Fruit of the Spirit* within her.

167

Several transitions take place in this verse. She boldly used the word Lover to describe her intimate mate, who is the passion of her life. Also, there's a shift from His needing to ask her to do something. Now, she welcomes Him to accomplish His desires in her life. New stability, assurance, and victory are evident in the Bride's voice. There is no fear because all her confidence is in the One she loves.

I have come into My garden, My sister, My Bride; I have gathered My myrrh with My spice. I have eaten My honeycomb and My honey; I have drunk My wine and My milk. (5:1)

The word "My" appears nine times in this verse. Each time He spoke the word, "My" He declared He has been allowed another level of ownership.[4]

She has *died to the flesh and been filled with Christ,* (Galatians 4:4) *the fullness of Him who fills all in all.* (Ephesians 1:23) *In Him she has been made complete.* (Colossians 2:10)

The Bride collected spices (Jesus's virtues) in the dark places of trials and test, where he once led her. He declared His joy in her sweetness (honey), strength (wine), and the richness of His Word (milk) within her.

Scripture: *He will give you the treasures of darkness, riches stored in secret places.* (Isaiah 45:3)

... He brings forth the wind from His storehouses. (Jeremiah 51:16)

... He walks upon the wings of the wind; He makes the winds His messengers ... (Psalm 104:3-4)

Prayer: Lord, the Bride wanted You so completely she asked for winds to test her. I guess I too will come to a time when I ask for the trials and testing of your winds. I can't imagine that right now, but help me so I won't hesitate or draw back from all you want for me. Fill me so full of Your Holy Spirit I can faithfully stand against anything that blasts me. Help me be willing to follow You to deep dark places so I can be one who pleases You. Thank You for loving me so much.

My Revelation:

Inviting Friends

Eat, O friends, and drink: drink your fill, O Lovers (5:1)

During the enjoyment of their honeymoon, the Bridegroom decided to show off His Bride to others. This verse is similar to when God said to Satan, *Have you seen my servant Job, for there is no one like him on the earth, a blameless and upright man* (Job 1:8). God is inviting all of heaven, earth, and hell to check out His Bride.

He's saying, *taste, and see, that the Lord is good.* (Psalm 34:8) The time has come for others to be invited to see what perfection looks like.

Lovers would be those closest to Him. So first, Jesus invited the Holy Family to enjoy the finished work. This would be the same as when newlyweds welcome their relatives to a housewarming party once their new home is ready for company.

He also invited friends to eat. When our inner man (soul) belongs totally to God, He has the liberty of choosing whoever He wants to come and enjoy what is His. However, Jesus's choice of friends may not necessarily be who we would choose. It's challenging to have Him welcome others into our life. They're not necessarily like Him. They can be ungrateful and rude. Sometimes those guests trample through our garden and try all the fruit. They test patience, endurance, peace, and the ability to stay sweet when others act ugly.

People are starving for God's truth, light, and life. He wants to give His Bride, and all she is to others. As He welcomes difficult people into our life it can feel as if they suck everything good out of us. That is true because they draw on Jesus's goodness within us.

Personally, feeding people Jesus's love, hope, and encouragement often exhausted me. In helping them fight their spiritual enemies, I sometimes came away needing a gasp of clean spiritual air, and receive a fresh cleansing of Jesus's blood. But, our high call is to share His fruit with others, so I needed to learn how to grow a new crop. All that was necessary was to follow Jesus's pattern. We draw away and plug into the Holy Spirit, our power source, and recharge. We come away and rest in Jesus's arms where we find His fresh anointing, strength, and energy. Once refilled, we're ready for the next opportunity to share Him with others. As we stay in the steps of the Spirit, there's the rhythm of giving out, and of pulling away to recharge as He leads.

Scripture: *Greater love has no one than this that one lay down his life for his friends.* (John 15:10)

Be fruitful and multiply ... (Genesis 1:18)

Walk in a manner worthy of the Lord to please Him in all respects, bearing fruit in every good work ... (Colossians 1:10)

Jesus said ... *Do you love Me? Feed My sheep.* (Matthew 25:41)

... Truly I say to you, to the extent that you did it to one of these brothers of Mine, even the least of them, you did it to Me. (Matthew. 25:41)

Prayer: Jesus, it's lovely to think of You finding pleasure in the garden of my soul, and inviting the Father and the Holy Spirit to join us. Welcome.

You chose some unusual sinner friends while on earth, and You haven't changed. Help me welcome them as freely as I've welcomed You. I choose to give Your love, and all good things to others, just as I would You. I will try to follow Your leading as You tell me to withdraw and recharge, and when You tell me to move out to touch others. What a wonderful privilege to be Your vessel for the world.

My Revelation:

The Testing

I slept but my heart was awake. Listen! My Lover is knocking. Open to Me, My sister, My darling, My dove, My flawless one. (5:2)

After much ministry, for that's what sharing fruit is, the Bride rested. Her spirit constantly listened for her Lover's call. She heard Him knock, wanting to enter. Strange, He's always welcome to be in her garden, but for some reason, this time He asked her permission to enter. Evidently, something new is about to take place.

This tapping could be described personally as feeling a new pull, or an unsettling. For me, when He draws, my spirit becomes alert, as if change is in the air. Not wanting to miss what He's doing, I seek understanding. However, it doesn't always come quickly, and I've learned the hard way it doesn't help to run ahead and try to figure everything out. Instead, in the waiting time, I must quiet myself, search my heart for the ever-attacking fear of the unknown, and listen for the Holy Spirit's leading. I whisper, "Lord, You've got my attention. Show me Your will."

Even while sleeping, my spirit is tuned to hear Him say, *this is the way, walk in it.* (Isaiah 30:21)

The Bride has been enjoying the glorious feeling of being clean from crown to toe while covered in her robe of righteous. She's content with their garden fellowship, and finds delight in having fruit usable for His purposes. Completely satisfied with their relationship, she sensed if she opened to His nudge, she might have to face some dark unknown thing. She stretched in her bed, as if giving the opportunity some thought, turned over, relaxed, and lingered.

She's always free to say no and stay put. If she does, she can continue to feed others God's fruit from her life. Many have stayed at this place in their spiritual journey, and others have been helped by the blessings of their sacrifices. Such service is noble and won't require the misery that comes with what He offers now.

As the Bride matures, there are many times she faces Revelation 3:20. *I stand at the door and knock and if anyone hears My voice and opens I will come in and sup with them and them with Me.*

Today's verse describes one of those times, but she was pretty sure something undesirable would be required if she opened, so she let Him knock. And she's right. In fact, because the Lord knew accepting this challenge would be difficult, He lovingly emphasized the word *My* four times to remind her of His ownership.

Of course, we know the Lover was so close He is really laying right beside her as He asked to be trusted enough to open her soul even more fully to the mysteries of the Spirit. His request will be so impossible for her, He just as well ask her to voluntarily stop breathing. But all He wants is for her to be willing. The Holy Spirit will accomplish everything else.

The Bridegroom's desire is asking for entrance into the very center of her soul's universe. Eternal places where there's no limitation.

The size of our spirit is infinite, and was created to have full authority over our soul. As humans, we have a soul (mind, will, and emotions), a body, and a spirit. However, God's plan was for us to be spirit humans with a soul and a body. When the Holy Spirit owns our life completely, our spirit is empowered with the maturity to rule our soul. We'll think with the mind of Christ. Seeking His help, we'll yield to Kingdom attitudes and become free from unholy emotions. Then our body can align with the power of the Word, which brings divine health to our body. God has much to teach us about living in health.

When the Bride's spirit, united with the Holy Spirit, owns her soul, expansion the size of God's Kingdom will happen in her life.

Once again, the Lover has gone deep into His garden and found things in her which haven't been opened to Him. Not places she withheld, but areas she doesn't know exist. If she's willing, He will pour life into the new unknown places so deep within her soul they are beyond measure. Truly, they hadn't evolved before the Spirit was given freedom to renew her, expand her rooms, and open new areas.

By the Lord's loving tones, the Bride understood Him to say, "Rise up, my fair one, come and suffer with Me."

Yes, He's ready to share with her *the fellowship of His suffering* (Philippians 3:10) *for we are made perfect through suffering,* (Hebrews 2:10) *and it is to the degree that we share in the suffering of Christ that we also rejoice at the revelation of His glory.* (I Peter 4:13)

What awful sounding verses. *The testing* is the hardest part of Song of Solomon to write. No one would want to follow into the fullness of God if they knew the truth of these verses. This new enticement is beyond possibility. It's the call of the martyrs.

Martyrs are those who've found the fulfillment of love, and willingly lay their lives down for a friend. (John 15:13) Love owns them so completely they've surrendered all thoughts of hanging onto their lives. They've chosen the day they die by giving their will totally to God. If life were required, they would fearlessly step into Jesus's glorious arms and continue living in His Kingdom. God longs for us to become so familiar with His glory realm that when we leave this life, we'll know we're home. The change should cause no more disruption to us than when we step from a solid floor onto an escalator.

That He would grant you, according to the riches of His glory, to be strengthened with power through His Spirit in the inner man; so that Christ may dwell in your hearts through faith; and that you, being rooted and grounded in love, may be able to comprehend with all the saints what is the breadth and length and height and depth, and to know the love of Christ which surpasses knowledge that you may be filled up to all the fullness of God. (Ephesians 3:16-19)

Paul chose this call and said, *I have been crucified with Christ; and it is no longer I who live, but Christ lives in me; and the life which I now live in the flesh I live by faith in the Son of God, who loved me, and delivered Himself up* for me. (Galatians 2:20)

The heart of the martyr wants nothing of this world. Their bodies serve here for Kingdom purposes as their spirits unite with God. They have clear vision of earth from heaven, (Revelation 3:21) and see Jesus face to face.

People we would give the title martyr today are those who suffer around the world to help others come to know Jesus's love. They boldly carry God's kingdom into dangerous countries. They lay down their lives daily. Many die without anyone knowing the loss of a great saint, but their reward is sweet.

Revelation 6:9-11 tells us that under the altar of the throne of God are *the souls of all who had been martyred for the Word of God and for being faithful in their testimony ... a white robe was given to each of them. And they were told to rest a little longer until the full number of their brothers and sisters their fellow servants of Jesus who were to be martyred – had joined them.*

If the Bride is willing to endure what she perceives to be more testing, the Holy Spirit will be there to carry her in His strength, love, and wisdom.

This call is asking the Bride to give her Beloved her very humanness and God-given drive to survive.

Incredible.

Scripture: ... *May your spirit and soul and body be preserved complete, without blame at the coming of our Lord Jesus Christ.* (I Thessaliens 5:23)

I determine to know nothing among you except Jesus Christ and Him crucified. (I Corinthians 2:2)

For it was fitting for Him, for whom are all things, and through whom are all things, in bringing many sons to glory, to perfect the author of their salvation through suffering. (Hebrews 2:10)

We are afflicted in every way, but not crushed; perplexed, but not despairing; persecuted, but not forsaken; struck down, but not destroyed; always carrying about in the body the dying of Jesus, that the life of Jesus also may be manifested in our body. For we who live are constantly being delivered over to death for Jesus's sake, that the life of Jesus also may be manifested in our mortal flesh. So death works in us, but life in you. (II Corinthians 4:8-12)

For momentary, light affliction is producing for us an eternal weight of glory far beyond all comparison. (II Corinthians 4:17)

Prayer: Lord, You are knocking to see if I'll willingly open to unknown things. I'm having trouble even believing this is a possibility. I thought serving others was our ultimate goal.

Did You really plan for my spirit to be so alive, it dominates my mind, will, and emotions, and even rules my body with divine health?

I can't die to being human, or voluntarily stop breathing, can I? Free me again from fear of the unknown. I feel stretched too far. No wonder the bride let You wait. You know I don't want to suffer, and I have no desire to be a martyr. But You seem to want to expand my faith even more, so I can know Your more excellent way.

I repent of wanting to hide and stay contentedly where I am. I must remember Your faithfulness, and Your unusual ways of doing things. I'm also sure You are a good God with only good, perfect things for me. And Your love, Your wonderful love, is better than any of my concerns of death. So I'll take Your challenge and say, "Yes Lord" to choosing the day I die. Let Your love destroy all my fear so I can embrace the call of the martyr. Thank You for revealing You want Your eternal weight of glory to own my life through suffering.

My Revelation:

He Waits

My head is filled with dew and my hair with the dampness of the night. **(5:2)**

The Lord never forces anyone to follow Him. He only knocks and asks. Then He quietly waits until someone is ready to receive Him. He is so long-suffering He remains until His head is filled with dew. Jesus has been waiting for us to want Him above everything else for a really long time.

I have taken off my robe—must I put it on again? I have washed my feet—must I soil them again? **(5:3)**

As the Holy Spirit drew the Bride to experience more, it's no wonder she couldn't understand what He was asking of her. She thought about the impure robe of self-righteousness she laid aside. Does He want her to put it on again? He knows people are watching His purity in her life.

These questions aren't because of disobedience. She's seeking understanding just as Peter did when God told Him to eat unholy meat. (Acts 10:14) After all, He has wanted her to do some very confusing things in the past.

But, the truth is, she is ready for a promotion. He wants to take her to even higher places.

Anytime we choose to be different by stepping out of the normal human mold, we will be persecuted. The little bit of suffering she's known in the past came with admiration and approval, as people seemed to appreciate her sacrifice. This time she sensed if she followed into more suffering with Him, family members and mentors would be upset and strongly disapprove, knowing such a call to be unsafe. How could they understand why she would foolishly consider such a thought?

Yes, they are right, for this is the high call that sends healthy people into impossible situation. Those with great potential in successful careers choose to go into dangerous inner cities to serve others who are hurting. Some secretly go into a country to boldly win a nation to Jesus where terrorists enjoy killing saints. This call moves people from thriving ministries into isolation to reach one little untouched tribe in some far away country no one seems to know exists. The call of a martyr is truly dying a deeper death.

God starts teaching us to suffer in little ways. Like when He wakes me in the middle of a cold winter night, asking me to suffer by getting up to pray. I love my warm bed so much I decide it would be better to pray in bed. Instead, I'm back to sleep in ten moments.

Or perhaps, when He whispers to me to give up food for a day, and I decide it would be okay if I just didn't eat junk food as a fast instead.

Then there are times when He says, "Come away and be alone with me." I try so hard. But after about three hours I think of a hundred things needing attention. Some of them are even good works, so I go on my way. The call to suffer for Christ's sake doesn't come easy.

However, because the Bride wears His righteous robe now, and her feet are clean (purity), He will continue to call her to this deeper level. All He wants to hear His humble Bride say is, "Yes Lord." He will do the rest.

And remember one more thing about being tested. Before going any higher with God, the old tormentors who once bound us will come around again. Scripture says when demons are cast out they'll come back and bring others with them to see if there's any place in our soul unattended. They check for any weakness in our flesh that might be open to evil temptation. (Luke 11:26)

When our house has been swept clean the tormentors still need a home, so they come to entice us with the same things that once held us in bondage.

How do we respond when fear raises its ugly head again? Do we fall when a misunderstanding hurts our feelings? Does worry win when the checkbook shows a $2.00 balance? These tests are allowed to see if faith is established in areas where lack-of-faith once had a stronghold.

So, when it feels as if our peace has been stolen it could be the enemy of our soul has swooped by with a test to see if there is any entry to trespass into our spiritual house. When this happens, we are to stay filled with the Holy Spirit, declare victory, praise Jesus, and they'll move on.

This is what the Bride is experiencing. In her case *obedience without question* has been challenged.

Scripture: ... *turn to the Lord, be obedient unto His voice.* (Deuteronomy 4:30)

If you consent and obey you will eat the best of the land. (Isaiah 1:19)

Prayer: Lord, the title, *He Waits,* makes me question how much I've made You wait for me. Forgive me, Lord. I realize Your call isn't to prepare me for a lovely flesh life, but for a spirit-life of supernatural power and glory that makes my earthly-life seem trivial. Thank You for the tests You allow. I ask for discernment to recognize when the enemy comes to test areas where I already have victory. I love and follow You, Lord.

My Revelation:

The Day to Die

My Lover thrust His hand through the latch-opening; my heart began to pound for Him. (5:4)

The Bride bravely said yes again. All she knew to do in obedience was to have a willing heart. By revelation, she's aware the Holy Spirit is drawing her to open herself to Him in new unknown ways. *He stuck His hand through the latch* means He reached inside her soul to unbolt places where He had been kept out.

When God reveals His supernatural plans to us in detail, we are overwhelmed. Job said, *"Have pity on me, my friends, for the hand of God has touched me."* (Job 19:21) As we experience our Lover's God-sized passion, we also come to know Him as a wonderful, terrible God. He is wonderful in every way, yet terrible to behold in His majesty and power. Just a portion of His might is revealed in this verse from Isaiah 40:15. *The nations are like a drop from a bucket, and are regarded as a speck of dust on the scales; Behold, He lifts up the islands like fine dust.*

By the time we reach this place in our walk with God we no longer need to ask Him to show us the fullness of His plans. We recognize we have been allowed the privilege of the title martyr. We don't need to know anymore.

We are only given enough grace and mercy for today. He will hold the rest of our days for us. Our heart understands whatever the future brings, it's too big and wonderful to look at right now.

Also, we're far past having pride or ego stroked from being used by God. It's with holy fear and a trembling heart we endeavor to follow His leading by faith in Him. We know nothing can be of ourselves or we will fail miserably.

My thoughts are nothing like your thoughts, says the Lord. And My ways are far beyond anything you can imagine. (Isaiah 55:8)

I arose to open for my Lover, my hands dripped with myrrh, my fingers with flowing myrrh, on the handles of the lock. (5:5)

As she opened to her Lover her hands (strength, power, actions and possessions) were filled with willingness to surrender to suffering (myrrh). Her fingers (works[5]) moved forward as she gave up her natural desire to survive.

Longing for her Lord overcame every thought of caution. She broke free (she arose) and yielded to Him with new anticipation of His presence. The Bride chose to put *self-preservation,* and her natural *will to live* into the hands of God. Those traits have

190

kept her safe many times, and are the last places in her soul to be unlocked. Death can no longer hold her captive.

She stepped into the life of Galatians 2:20.

I have been crucified with Christ and I no longer live, but Christ lives in me. The life I live in the body, I live by faith in the Son of God, who loved me and gave Himself for me ...

When we live what this verse describes we will move into God so completely our physical life will no longer holds us captive. We can choose to die right now, and if a day comes when we're required to stand with the martyrs, we'll shine in God's glory as His witnesses, and cross over into our next life with only the words Stephen spoke on our lips. *Lord, do not hold this sin against them.* (Acts 7:60)

Scripture: *Behold the kindness and severity of God ...* (Romans 11:22)

... Besides You, I desire nothing on earth. (Psalm 73:25)

Prayer: Thank You, for revelation Lord. I have no understanding as to how suffering can be a victorious treasure. We fight so hard for self-preservation. Our will to live is strong. I find it difficult to think of giving up control of myself totally to You. But if I don't, I may never really live fully. Please continue to reveal the mysteries of the privilege of suffering for Your sake, and choosing the day I die.

Help me love so fully that if it's ever required, I can pray Stephen's prayer, too. In fact, right now I pray You hold no sin against anyone who has hurt me. I choose to forgive them.

My Revelation:

He is Gone

I opened for my Lover, but My Lover had left; He was gone. My heart sank at His departure. I looked for Him but did not find Him. I called Him but He did not answer. (5:6)

He was Gone. No greater words of agony can come from a heart totally sold out to God. The Bride has given up everything. All she has left in her heart is love for Him. Her only desire is the delight of hearing His voice and the joy of His presence. She longed to feel the comfort of His loving arms surrounding her. That's all she wanted or needed. But He's gone.

I understand a little bit the total emptiness of the Bride. She felt as if she were a hollow shell where He once lived. Her mind was blank because she had learned to think with the mind of Christ. Before, the Holy Spirit was always with her to guide her steps, and to remind her of the truth of the Word. There is no greater suffering than knowing God's presence intimately, and then have it lift from you. Jesus's suffering was devastating when His Father turned from Him. (Matthew 27:46)

She looked for Him (she meditated) and called to Him (she prayed). Her heart sank in despair.

The watchmen found me as they made their rounds in the city. They beat me, they bruised me; they took away my shawl, those watchmen of the walls! (5:7)

Watchmen represent her previous mentors who helped with her spiritual maturity. Their responsible was to watch over the city and its people, so they found her.

Those who cared about her told her she paid too high a price for her Christianity. They said she had gone overboard (bruised), and become radical in her passion for Jesus.

After experiencing their attacks (beat), she couldn't even pray because they took her prayer shawl.

Just as God allowed Satan to sift Job, (Job 1:8) our purity will be tried. The persecutors can be men or demons, and there will seem to be no logic to the trials. The battles will be less fierce if we recognize our persecutor is always Satan; not people. It is the enemy who sifts us, no matter what form the watchman takes.

When I was misunderstood, even attacked by people I loved, it was hurtful. The pain was even worse when I felt God turned His back on me. During those trials, I couldn't hear His words of love anymore, and I questioned why the Holy Spirit wasn't guiding me. Before, His voice was a natural

194

part of my life. His presence created the joy of my existence. But during the time God was silent, I felt alone, empty, and emotionless.

People don't understand seeking a Lover from another realm, but I knew if I didn't find Him again I would surely die.

A lovesick person does strange things, but this verse describes even more than being lovesick. Before, the Beloved declared His bride ravished His heart. At the time this seemed too wonderful and amazing to believe. Knowing such love as a possibility, planted a seed in her heart that grew. A question began to burn, "Do I have a heart ravished for God, as His heart is for me?" At the beginning of chapter five the answer would have been no. She did love Him with all her heart, soul, strength, and mind (Matthew 22:37), but her love for Him was not the eat-me-alive, die-for kind of love ravished implied.

She knew she wanted to love God as He loves her. Truthfully, she only loved Him at all because He loved her first. (I John 4:19) This is the Bride's new calling, to have a ravished heart for God. Few find this love. Some don't even want it.

The torment of the perceived absence of the Lover stretched her heart to expand with love. Yes, she even became *ravished* for Him. She didn't know how desperately in love she would become when she opened the door and found He was gone.[1]

Miraculously, because of such loss, she can express new depths of passion for her Bridegroom. Love seeps through her pores, and floats on her breath. She's infectious to people around her. Others fall under conviction in her holy presence. They seem caught by the divine magnetic pull of the Holy Spirit as He draws them to know the same passion.

O daughters of Jerusalem, I charge you—if you find my Lover, what will you tell Him? Tell Him I am faint with love. **(5:8)**

In despair, the Bride thought it possible the daughters might find her Lover before she did. She remembered how gently He led her when they first met. Maybe, the daughters know Him in the same sweetness now.[1]

Passion's desperation overtook the Bride. Her ravished love called out, "Tell Him ..."

Faithfully, the Holy Spirit responded, and encompassed her more fully than ever before. Waves of glory pulsated through her body, and her expanded heart filled with God's love.

With the power of the supernatural experience more glorious transformation evolved. Complete restoration and the excitement for a divine life became so powerful she hardly recognized herself. A question developed, "What was she to do with Love's fullness in her of life?" She cried out to the daughters, "Tell Him," or "Help God!"

The bubbling, bubbling glory within her needed to find an outlet. When she opened her mouth she spoke loving words to everyone. Those expressions weren't always socially acceptable as she broke through society's barriers and exposed her passionate heart to strangers foolishly in public places. She loved them as much as she loved Jesus.

Joy burst forth. Filled with such happiness, she laughed too loudly. She was so full of energy she couldn't sleep. What's a girl to do when the Kingdom of Love owns her flesh?

How is your Beloved better than others, most fairest (or beautiful) of women? How is your Beloved better than others, that you charge us so? (5:9)

All she told the daughters was she was faint with love. But they saw more in her passion and desperation for Him. The beauty of humility, holiness (fairest), and the glory, joy and love of the Bride stirred their souls. So, as only the Holy Spirit can accomplish, hunger drew the daughter's hearts, and He made a way for this Bride of passion to describe her Beloved.

Scripture: *The earth groans for the sons of God to be revealed.* (Romans 8:22)

... *He who began a good work in me will be faithful to complete it.* (Philippians 1:6)

Prayer: I'm having trouble realizing Your heart is ravished with love for me, and now I see my love for You is to grow to be ravished as well. Oh my, I feel like such a baby in this Christian life. Lord, let Your Kingdom love own me. Thank You for the promise, You will finish the good work You began in me.

My Revelation:

Divine Revelation

The daughters asked the question. "What kind of beloved is yours?"

The Bride needed to transcend human comprehension to describe the One she loves. How does she explain her God, who is also her husband and friend? He isn't a flesh and blood human, but He is her spirit King from another realm. She'll try to describe His many-faceted character in a few carefully chosen words. Divine revelation flows from her loving lips as she speaks.

My Beloved is radiant and ruddy, outstanding among ten thousand. **(5:10)**

He is radiant, meaning He can't be compared to earth's humans. Her God-man shines. He's more brilliant than the sun; brighter than a nuclear blast. Seeing His glory would blind our natural eyes. Paul had that experience which is described in Acts 9:3-9.

The word ruddy means healthy and attractive. He's too radiant to look at, yet so lovely we don't want to take our eyes off Him. His appearance exceeds the greatest work of art ever created, or the most breathtaking scene found in our world. He is splendid.

Ten prophetically describes divine order and perfection. Thousand is divine completeness, an indefinite large number. He is outstanding among all others. Divine perfection.[1]

His head is purest gold; His hair is wavy and black as a raven. His eyes are like doves by the water streams, washed in milk, mounted like jewels. **(5:11-12)**

He is Ruler (head) of the Kingdom of God (gold). His black hair tells us *He has the dew of youth.* (Psalms 110:3) His pure (doves) eyes have the ability to look into the depths of the soul. He knows us by His wisdom, knowledge (jewels) and understanding (milk). Nothing is hidden from His eyes.

She paused to reflect on His ways. *He sees me in depths no other can know. There's intimacy as He searches, and knows me. He watches when I sit and when I rise. Understands my thoughts. Scrutinizes my path. He is with me as I lay down. Intimately acquainted with all my ways. Even before there is a word on my tongue, He knows it all. He has enclosed me behind and before. Laid His hand upon me. This knowledge is too wonderful for me. It's too high. I cannot understand it.* (Psalm 139:1-6)

His cheeks are like beds of spice yielding perfume. His lips are like lilies dripping with myrrh. (5:13)

Cheeks represent the soul[5] (mind, will, and emotion). Knowing the fragrance of Jesus's character overwhelmed her. His virtues carry the perfume of Kingdom spices which haven't been adulterated by anything of earth, so they intoxicate with inexpressible ecstasy.

Grace pours from His lips (Psalms 45:2). His words are surrounded by the splendor of His pure (lilies), sacrificial (dripping myrrh) love.

His arms are rods of gold set with topaz. His body is like polished ivory decorated with sapphires. (5:14)

Arms represent the strength and power of authority (rods) in the Kingdom of God (gold) in all of His beauty (topaz).[5]

His body is our perfect sacrifice (ivory) intertwined with heaven's glory (sapphire). Ivory was considered a precious treasure, but to own its beauty an elephant had to suffer or die. She prophetically told the daughters, Jesus, as their most precious treasure, will give His life for them.

His legs are pillars of marble set on bases of pure gold. His appearance is like Lebanon, choice as its cedars. (5:15)

Imagine the daughters hearing this prophetic description of the King. Their mouths would probably be hanging open in awe.

The Bride reflected on the rapturous times she spent with her King as she continued.

"His strength (legs) and power (pillars) are a firm foundation (bases) of the Kingdom (gold). Lebanon represents the land between Heaven and earth. He reigns above all others just as the tall cedar tree in the forest.

His mouth is sweetness itself; He is wholly desirable. This is my Lover, and this is my Friend, O daughters of Jerusalem. (5:16)

The bride is a woman who knows her man. As she revealed who her Bridegroom was in intimate detail, she too received even more understanding of her extraordinary Lover, because in truth, it was the Holy Spirit describing Him through her.

When she spoke of His mouth being full of sweetness, she realized she *knows* His kisses. In the beginning she'd asked Him to kiss her with the kisses of His lips (1:2). Somehow, beyond her ability to explain, Jesus moved past the veil between heaven and earth, and made what seemed impossible, possible. She knows the reality of His passionate touch (kisses) of love.

After trying to describe the One who is indescribable, she realized her heart was ravished for Him. Her words became perfect in description and simplicity as she paused and then said, "He is wholly desirable."

Knowing complete fulfillment and satisfaction in Him, she finished by simply sharing, "I know His kisses, and they are sweet. He's all love. Perfect! He's my Lover, my Friend."

This is the climax of Song of Solomon. The Bride *knows* God. In ravished love, she declared the fusion of being One with her Beloved.

The closest we flesh people know the intimacy described here is our God-given sexual passion. It was God's plan for man and woman to find heavenly fulfillment in their lives together by experiencing the satisfaction of marital sex. He wanted us to know physically the fiery intensity of the love He has for us spiritually. He longs for Spirit to spirit communion with His Bride.

We are aware sex can be defiled when flesh drives passion instead of God's love bringing true fulfillment. Selfishness and lust steal the treasure of human sexuality. Satan's perversion blinds hearts to

God's gift with distortion which ruins the beauty, love, and purity God planned.

But Jesus is a great redeemer. He knows how to restore relationships, and is willing to bring love, purity and pleasure back into the bedrooms. He has amazing power to free people from the past, giving them a clean slate so they can establish new trust and freedom together.

Scripture: *There is no one like You among the God's, O Lord; nor are there any works like Yours. All nations whom You have made shall come and worship before You and they shall glorify Your name. For You are great and do wondrous deeds; You alone are God.* (Psalms 86:8-10)

Prayer: Lord, Thank You, for a glimpse of Your majesty in these verses. You are glorious beyond understanding. It's hard to grasp You want spiritual intimacy with us which is more powerful than the emotions of a sexual relationship. I invite you to open my spirit to receive whatever's needed to find the fulfillment of a Spirit to spirit bond with You. I don't want to miss anything You have for me, so again I say, "Yes Lord."

:

The Victory

Where has your Lover gone, most beautiful of women? Which way did your Lover turn that we may look for Him with you? (6:1)

Sinners and saint's faith comes alive when the wonder of God's love and goodness is shared. Fresh testimonies of experiences with Him in His power and presence have the same effect as a spark of fire on dry kindling. They burn with vibrant light.

Finding words to demystify the supernatural glory of the Kingdom of God is so challenging. It seems impossible to explain the feelings of having Jesus's arms wrapped around you when there is no one physically near, or describe the gratification of dancing with Him in the Spirit, sometimes without even moving. How do we share communing with our God, who lives in another realm, for great lengths of time without a word being spoken? And yet, in that silence we receive new vision and understanding. These things are just too hard to make perfectly clear.

The Bride agreed with Paul's words, *None of these things move me because I count all things but loss for the excellence of the knowledge of Christ Jesus my Lord: for whom I suffered the loss of all*

*things, and count them but refuse, that I may gain
Christ, and be found in Him, not having a
righteousness of my own. That I may be clothed in
righteousness from God through faith in Jesus
Christ. I gladly suffer the loss of all things that I may
know Him, and the power of His resurrection, and
the fellowship of His sufferings, becoming conformed
to His death; that when He comes for His bride, I
may attain to the resurrection from the dead.*
(Philippians 3:7-11)

**My Lover has gone down to His garden, to the
beds of spices, to browse in the gardens and to
gather lilies. (6:2)**

After the Bride finished her testimony of the
King's beauty she realized where He was. He
promised He would never leave her or forsake her.
(Hebrews 13:5) In truth, He was with her all the
time. She remembered her garden still belonged to
Him. (4:16, 5:1) *The Lord is near her, even in her
mouth and in her heart.* (Deuteronomy 30:4) She felt
as if He left her, but in reality He was deeper within
her soul enjoying her virtues (spices) and purity
(lilies).

**I am my Lover's and my Lover is mine; He feeds
among the lilies. (6:3)**

With new understanding of His promise to always be with her, the Bride realized she doesn't always need to feel God's presence to know she is totally absorbed in Him. New freedom came in knowing what she feels or thinks is immaterial to the fact God's all-consuming presence is always in her life. There's no longer any reason for strife. She loves Him with passionate holy love just as He loves her. The two have become One. She has found rock solid faith which also brings contentment.

Before, in verse 2:2 the Bridegroom was described as gathering her purity (lilies), now we are told He feeds upon His own purity within her. He called her to supper when He stood at the door and knocked. (Revelation 3:20) He prepared supper (His fruit and virtues) as the Holy Spirit did His work of perfection within the garden of her soul. Then, He became the true nourishment of her life (Supper) as He lived in her, and dined with her.

Scripture: *The glory which You have given Me I have given to them; that they may be one, just as We are one. I in them, and You in Me that they may be perfected in unity ...* (John 17:22-23)

Prayer: Thank You, Lord that You live in me, and I am victorious in You. Let this amazing reality own my heart. Lord, help me freely share Your love and

freedom with others. I need to know how to express
Your wonderful ways more fully.

My Revelation:

Unity

God's truth freed the Bride to hear her Beloved's words of love again. Now, He describes the beauty He sees in the unity of all God's people as His Bride. Just as our Bridegroom is one, yet part of the Trinity of God, Jesus's Bride is one made up of billions of sold-out lovers united in Him. She has become more than His warrior bride, she is a supernatural military force moving together to take nations for the Kingdom of God.

In these verses we hear what the multiplicity of the finished work of the Bride looks like.

You are beautiful, My darling, as Tirzah, lovely as Jerusalem, majestic as troops with banners. **(6:3-4)**

Tirzah was chosen as the royal city for the kings of Canaan. A place is a ghost town without people, so the city's name represents the beauty of the saints living in the glory of God.

Jesus has always loved Jerusalem, and the Bride is just as precious to Him.

You are the light of the world. A city set on a hill cannot be hidden ... let your light shine before men that they may see your good works, and glorify your Father who is in heaven. (Matthew 5:14, 16)

Describing the united army as majestic reminds me of the splendor of the Rocky Mountains. They overwhelm us with their massive beauty long before we get close. When driving into them, it's as if we're captured by their magnificence.

In the same way, the troops appear as glorious peaks on the horizon. They move across the land in united Kingdom power engulfing everything with God's glory. Bringing restoration and righteousness everywhere blight and destruction once reigned.

Only He knows the outcome of unity's great power as they declare victory over every enemy. Even though I plan to be part of this army taking the land with Jesus, I shiver at the possibilities of such powerful unity.

The air is alive with electrifying currents of joy for victories won as banners fill the sky with floating colors. In Psalm 60:4 we read, *You have given a banner to them that fear You, that it may be displayed because of the truth.* Truth becomes victorious over lies and deception, which causes many in bondage to find freedom, a great conquest for God's champions.

The Bride takes the land by love. She has declared victory over their homes, cities, and nations.

Love is terrible and confusing to the enemy. Satan has no understanding of this secret weapon's power. The united Bride will cause his servants to cower in holes of darkness to escape the brilliance of the united Bride's light.

Turn your eyes from Me; they overwhelm Me. **(6:5)**

What a thought! God, who set the sun in the sky, and holds the ocean in His hand, (Isaiah 40:12) is so overwhelmed by the beauty of unity even He asked her to quit looking at Him. This verse is different from when He said she ravished His heart with one look of her eyes (4:9). She honored His call to seek His face, and the eyes of unity are a pure reflection of His holiness. Imagine the glory flashing from such a united Bride as billions of sets of pure holy eyes look into the face of Jesus. This overwhelms even the Trinity.

Your hair is like a flock of goats descending from Gilead. **(6:5)**

Her perpetual testimony (Gilead) shared in wisdom (hair[2]) flows on earth in covenant with the Kingdom.

The movement of the body of Christ is compared to a woman's hair. As she turns her head to follow

Jesus with her eyes, each strand of her hair moves together as a unit in response. The saints function as one, all staying in step with the Spirit's leading.

Your teeth are like a flock of sheep coming up from the washing. Each has its twin, not one of them is alone. **(6:6)**

Teeth prophetically indicate wisdom and understanding.[2] The Holy Spirit has brought the united Bride's mind, will, and emotions to absolute purity (washing). Each part of the Bride is perfectly attuned to the will of her Bridegroom. They work in unity just like teeth do. By studying (chew on) the truth of the Word as one, they are united in purpose.

The King tells us the Church has linked arms (twins), and is likeminded in understanding and wisdom, even though each person fulfills their unique call individually.

By unity, loneliness, which has no place in God's Kingdom, is destroyed. Instead, there is true fellowship, friendship, and family as every soul is valued and loved for the treasure they are. Real unity is always supernatural because it is only found in God.

God sets the solitary in families ... (Psalm 68:6)

The Bride of Christ, in holiness, has united and nothing she purposes to do will be impossible.

Scripture: *I have placed you as a light for the Gentiles that you should bring salvation to the ends of the earth.* (Acts 13:47)

Behold, how good and how pleasant it is for brothers to dwell together in unity. (Psalm 133:1)

Be diligent to preserve the unity of the Spirit in the bonds of peace. (Ephesians 4:3)

For then I will give to the people purified lips, that all of them may call on the name of the Lord, to serve Him shoulder to shoulder. (Zephaniah 3:9)

Prayer: Lord Jesus, Thank You, for this revelation. I want to be more united with the body of Christ, and become part of Your glorious army. Come Holy Spirit, let Your unity reign. Empower Your people in holiness and purpose so our nations can be transformed in righteousness. Thank You, loneliness has no place in Your Kingdom. You want us to destroy it by sharing Your love.

My Revelation:

Unity II

Your temples behind your veil are like the halves of pomegranate. (6:7)

The Bride, as many people, is as abundant as seeds in a pomegranate. Their thoughts are open (halves), and in unity with the Holy Spirit's thinking. With wisdom and understanding, they are able to complete all God has planned for the hour. The power of unity makes everything so much easier. There's agreement in the most effective ways to accomplish projects, with no wasted effort or emotions from people thinking they have a better idea. Everyone has supernatural clarity on how to link arms to accomplish tasks quickly and powerfully.

As Oneness takes place on earth, things change. Governments make righteous choices as the Holy Spirit anoints people with His authority to serve. Holiness takes the airwaves. The Bible is on every teacher's desk as a reference for all subjects. Supernatural unity brings great transformation.

Sixty queens there may be, and eighty concubines and virgins beyond number (6:8)

215

God is sitting on His Throne in heaven with Jesus at His right hand watching His Bride come together. The Holy Spirit has opened the ears of His people to hear, their eyes to see, and given them hearts that understand. The God of the universe is directing the greatest orchestration of yielded humanity in history.

Solomon was overwhelmed by God's heart as he shared his revelation. He declared, "I see the royal Queen bearing all of God's virtues (sixty is completeness[2]). They are the people who have laid down their lives to belong to the King. He loves them. I hear the concubine's (not legally married[1]) voices of praise and testimony (eighty is speech or mouth[2]). Masses of pure saints (virgins) are coming to Him and He is overjoyed."

But My dove, My perfect one, (6:9)

The Bride as One has found perfection. The Word told her to *be perfect as He is perfect* (I Peter 1:16), but she thought it impossible. However, with the Bride's surrender and more surrender, trial after more trials, dying and more dying, she is now called His pure (dove) perfect one. The body united in Christ is holy and righteous, completing Brother Lawrence's formula *none of self, all of God.*[6]

Billions of humans, perfected in holiness and filled with the glory of God, are united with the King of kings because God's ravished love has been allowed to own them.

Scripture: *The glory which You have given me I have given to them; that they may be one, even as We are One, I in them and You in Me that they may be perfect in unity.* (John 17:22-23)

I exhort you, brethren, by the name of our Lord Jesus Christ, that you all agree, and there be no divisions among you, but that you be made complete in the same mind and in the same judgment.
(I Corinthians 1:10)

Prayer: Lord, we've never dreamed of really being united people. What a thought. This will truly take Your supernatural miracles. I'm being stretched again to think Your plan is Oneness and unity of the Believers. Let it be so, Lord Jesus.

My Revelation:

Unity III

The only daughter of her Mother, the favorite of the One who bore her. The daughters saw her and called her blessed; the queens and concubines praised her. (6:9)

The united Bride lives a blessed life, praised by all. She's the only daughter of the Holy Spirit (mother). The perfection of His completed work of love has brought great joy to the Trinity.

I remember when I was expecting my second child I was concerned I might not love the new baby as much as I loved the first. It felt as if all the motherly love in my heart belonged to her. However, when her little sister was born, I was amazed to find my heart seemed to expand, filling me with complete love for my second child too.

The Holy Spirit loves the Bride just as Father God, and Jesus the Bridegroom loves her. They have never given up on her finding the harmony of complete unity with herself and the Godhead.

The forerunners stretched themselves to know God. Through perseverance they found the power of unity, and they've blown spiritual trumpets that awakened a mighty sleeping giant ready to fulfill God's call.

We, who are many, are one body in Christ, and individually member's one of another. **(Romans 12:5)**

Who is this that grows like the dawn, fair as the moon, bright as the sun **(6:10)**

Solomon tells us the Trinity, united with the Bride, can be compared to the heavens. She's made up of multitudes of souls, just as the sky is filled with stars, the moon, and sun.

When this transformation is complete, our light will be the same as Jesus in Matthew 17:2. *His face shone like the sun, His garments became as white as light.* We, as His Bride united, represent the transcendent light of the glory realm. The more we're fully His, the brighter we'll shine with His glory. This brings terror to the enemy. Darkness can't bear God's holy light.

On earth the Bride is called *The Shining Ones.* Such radiance can't be hidden. Faces illuminate Kingdom glory shining from the inner-man. We glow.

This happens now. When in a crowd, I often see God's radiance in some of the faces. My spirit easily recognizes Jesus in them, and I'm drawn to their light.

I remember going to church after a trip to a spiritually dark nation. The darkness we'd experienced seemed to make my spirit-eyes extra sensitive to the brightness glowing from the spiritually alive saints who filled the church. I sat there looking at them in awe thinking, *I wonder if they have any idea how glorious they are.*

Light removes darkness. (Romans 13:12) The Bride, bearing light and love's unity, brings hope to the hearts of men, making it possible for people to receive forgiveness, acceptance, and love.

and terrible as a bannered host (or, majestic as stars in procession (6:10 NIV)

This verse is describing the Spirit realm. Jehovah Sabaoth, the Lord of Hosts has spoken. The Bride has made herself ready. By the Spirit's leading, the army of heaven moves forward with banners victoriously floating overhead.

Billions and billions of united angels descend to accomplish God's glorious purposes on earth. The Glory Holes of heaven, where angels ascend and descend from the throne of God, have been enlarged. Instead of stairs to heaven, a Highway of Holiness manifests. The Host of Heaven moves forward. No power on earth, or in hell, can slow them down.

I saw this glorious procession in a vision. The angel's appearance was like millions of moving lights in a huge spiral coming toward earth in power and oneness ready to unite with the Bride. The earth trembled from the force of the powerful, supernatural movement. Demons cowered knowing their time was up. They are too weak to fight the angels of God in unity with the Bride unified as One.

This scene was awesome and empowering to me as I recognized we're not alone in our battles. The angels have come with the authority to assist us in multiplied ways beyond anything imaginable.

Scripture: *You will become like blameless and pure children of God without fault in which you shine like stars in the universe as you hold out the Word of Life.* (Philippians 2:15)

Let your light shine before man in such a way that they will see your good works and glorify your Father in Heaven. (Matthew 5:16)

A highway will be there, a roadway, and it will be called the Highway of Holiness. (Isaiah 35:8)

The Kingdom of God is ever advancing and the violent take it by force. (Matthew 11:12)

Prayer: Lord, what amazing thoughts. Your plan is heaven and earth united in love and purpose. How have we missed all this? All I can say again is "Yes Lord." Come, Lord Jesus.

My Revelation:

The Harvest

The last few verses were like a piece of orchestrated music in grand finale as they revealed the body of Christ united. There's also a rhythmic flow as the Bridegroom continues.

I went down to the grove of nut trees, to look at the new growth in the valley, to see if the vines had budded or the pomegranates where in bloom. **(6:11)**

Jesus is moving on earth united with His Bride. They go to groves of nut trees (trees prophetically are nations[5]) and valleys (towns and cities). As He sweeps His hand across the horizon, new disciples awaken from their sleepy deception. They arise to join the great Kingdom warriors.

God is always about expansion, rescue, and redemption. He doesn't want one soul lost. The united ones are ready to win nations for their King.

He went to see if vines had budded for a new harvest of wine (strength and delight) so more can receive His House of Wine. He admired the young minds (pomegranates) who are prepared to receive His thoughts. He wants to fill them with His knowledge, wisdom, and understanding so He can plant divine ideas within them to revolutionize science, medicine, politics and business.

By unity, wherever Jesus goes, the Holy Spirit and the Bride gather.

Commandment number two, *love others as you love yourself* (Matthew 22:39), is the natural progression of loving God totally in obedience to His first commandment. The Bride is eager to help with His many gardens (souls), and excited to be part of the adventure He has planned.

As she goes through the land, people open their eyes to see Jesus is the One they've always wanted and they follow Him. She loves being wherever God's gardens (His people) are. Her delight is to help and love everyone just as God loves them.

Scripture: *Shepherd the flock of God among you, exercising oversight not under compulsion, but voluntarily, according to the will of God* ... (I Peter 5:2)

... the people will volunteer freely in the day of Your power; in holy array. (Psalm 110:3)

Prayer: Lord, Thank You for people who are willing to go wherever You lead them so others can know You. Free me from any hindrances that might be keeping me from fulfilling Your purposes for my life.

Help me move quickly when you say, "Go." I don't want to miss even one of the joys You have for me as I serve You.

My Revelation:

The Place of the Chariots

*Before I was aware, my soul set me over the
chariots of my noble people.* (6:12)

The Bride is enjoying partnership with God's
active glorious army when suddenly she's caught
away to the Kingdom. Psalm 68:17-18 tells us, *The
chariots of God are myriads, upon myriads; the Lord
is among them as He was in Sinai (*visible place of
God[1]*) and in the Holy Place. Thou hast ascended on
high, Thou hast led away captives ...*

Suddenly, without any new preparation, the
Bride enters *The Place of the Chariots.*[1] She isn't
asked to come away to this new place as in the past.
Being free from any earthly bonds, she's simple
caught away. Gravity has no hold on her.

We know the united Bride is many now, so this
could be the catching away of the whole body of
Christ which the church calls The Rapture.

But, I want to focus on the Bride as individuals
again so we can glean personally what God is saying.
Scripture tells us John was caught away in
Revelations 1:10, and Revelations 4:2. Also, Paul
wrote of being caught away in II Corinthians 12:2.
Both men were taken to heaven just as the Bride

was in this verse. God gave us the testimonies of faithful men in His Word to reveal we too can know these experiences personally. Surely, Solomon's revelation challenges our hearts to prepare for the unusual supernatural encounters God has planned for His Bride.

Just as the House of Wine was the place to receive our assignment, the Place of the Chariots is when God encompasses His Bride with power for service. She will ride in the glory of His anointed presence.

The saints have humbled themselves and prayed. They've purified their lives, sought His face, and walk in the steps of the Spirit (Galatians 5:25). Every person rests when He says rest, and they go out as He leads. Efforts to accomplish what they see the Father doing are supernatural as they move in the chariots of God. Man tries to understand their success. Their answer is always, "To God be the glory."

Signs, wonders, miracles, and the power to heal and deliver become normal for God's saints. By His manifest power masses of souls see the truth clearly. They shake off dullness and complacency, and march into the Kingdom of God by the Spirit's leading.

Supercharged saints accomplish in a moment what once took years. Abundant provision is available. Cities and governments are shaken to the core as righteousness stands up and declares truth. Law enforcement is unnecessary as evil bows to goodness.

People prefer one another, as the stronghold of selfishness is broken. The hearts of the fathers return to the children. A human life is recognized for its divine value. Hospitals are places of ministry, not surgery. God heals the sick through His saints. This is not a Pollyanna precept. God will move on the face of the earth. The hour is now.

I asked the Lord if I knew this place of the chariots. He showed me that although the chariots are literal and real in Heaven, our mode of transportation could look different in the visions the Holy Spirit chooses to use as our vehicle.

So, I was reminded of my images of rocket ships. My mind flipped back to years of mini-visions I'd experienced. There's no time or space in the Kingdom realm, therefore, the Holy Spirit often resumes a subject He started years ago. That's why I tell people to write this stuff down. Too often, I have to go back to old journals to review what He told me in the past, to grasp what He's trying to teach now.

My first rocket encounter came after a time of much spiritual growth. I felt such new maturity I thought I surely had it all together. In the first vision, I was standing in what appeared to be a missile silo where a giant rocket was in place. I stared at the massive powerful beast towering high above me. The Lord said, "See that tiny scratch on the side of the rocket?"

The mark on the shiny metal was so small I had to strain my eyes to see it.

"That's how much power you have."

Pride and arrogance deflated as I saw the speck that represented all I'd accomplished in trying so hard to grow spiritually. Humility wrapped me. I wilted as two more strongholds left.

After a few years of more maturing, I saw the rocket ship again. This time I was sitting inside looking at all the instruments. All I could think was, *Don't push any buttons.*

More maturing came and I experience another vision. The buttons had been pushed, and fire and smoky clouds powerfully bellowed from the boosters outside. The seat jiggled as the engines roared. It rumbled, and shook violently as it prepared to launch.

My last mini-vision a few years ago was blast off. I soared into the heavens, above the highest mountains, and into the quietness of the stars. Back on earth, I watched myself going into unknown places far, far away.

Power comes from getting into Him, His chariot, and going wherever it takes you.

Scripture: *The Kingdom of God does not consist of words, but in power.* (I Corinthians 4:2)

We have this treasure in earthen vessels that the surpassing greatness of the power may be of God and not from ourselves. (II Corinthians 4:7)

Humble yourself under the mighty hands of God that He may exalt you in due time. (I Peter 5:6)

Prayer: Lord, Your plan is for us to live on earth, and in heaven. I'm meant to live a power-filled life in You. Keep stretching me. I ask for more understanding and faith to grasp all You have for me. Help me recognize, and learn from the visions you give me. Remind me to journal my dreams. Help me perceive Your chariot, my mode of transportation into Your Kingdom. I realize it's really entering into You, but You seem to like to make these things fun for us. I love knowing You.

My Revelation:

Dance of Two Armies

Come back, come back, O Shulamite; come back, come back, that we may gaze on you! Why would you gaze on the Shulamite as on the dance before two armies (or a dance of Mahanaim?) (6:13)

The Bride is caught away in the chariot of God. For the first time she's called *Shulamite,* feminine for Solomon, meaning *daughter of peace.*[1] She's one with the *Prince of Peace.*

Only God's people know true peace. A worried, frustrated, frightened world longs to live in the powerful tranquility God's Bride has found. His Word says *the just and the unjust have the same trials,* (I Peter 3:18) but when believers walk calmly through challenges, people can see their faith. The virtue Peace gives evidence of His reality.

The daughters are attracted to God's glory in the Bride. They ask her to come back because by her light, they can see Jesus. This verse reveals the pull between earth and heaven, or flesh and the Spirit that is taking place. The Spirit says come away. The world beckons her to come back. These calls are like a war dance with each pulling the opposite direction.

235

Yes, we are being continually drawn to come to the Kingdom, and to stay on earth. Victory becomes reality when we break free from the flesh to live the life promised by the Spirit's call.

This is also a dance referring to Mahanaim.[1] The place Jacob saw as the entrance to heaven where angels ascend and descend from the throne of God. (Genesis 32:2) By revelation the daughters now see a victory dance of two armies as the united Bride, and the Hosts of Heaven, intertwine in the Holy Spirit's manifest presence.

The Spirit showed me this union of two realms was like two veils, one was white (Host of Heaven), the other red (the Bride of Christ). The veils moved and twirled together intertwining until they turned pink. The prayer, *Let Your Kingdom come and Your will be done on earth as it is in Heaven* (Matthew 6:10) was answered.

I've experienced this dance with the Spirit in times of worship. While sitting quietly, I saw myself in a white flowing gown with only the beauty of simplicity as adornment. I felt the twirling of a dance and was thrilled as the Holy Spirit's presence encircled me. I began to sing a simple little song.

Ribbons of glory dance 'round me
Ribbons of glory I see
Dancing and dancing and dancing

with Thee
Whirling and whirling 'round free
Ribbons of glory now wrap 'round me
Glory. And glory. And glory.

Scripture: *Sing to God, O Kingdoms of the earth,
sing praise to the Lord, to Him who rides upon the
highest heavens. Oh, God You are awesome from
Your sanctuary. He gives strength and power to the
people.* (Psalm 68:32-35)

*Holy, holy, holy, is the Lord of hosts, the whole earth
is full of His glory.* (Isaiah 6:3)

Prayer: Thank You, Lord for showing me You are
real, and I can dance with You. Amazing! I ask for
help to break free from my flesh so I can willingly
move with Your Spirit. I welcome the Host of
Heaven to intertwine with my life. Let me
experience ribbons of glory too, Lord. I long for
everything You have for me, and choose to be one
who brings peace.

My Revelation:

Forever

The couple has spent many hours of intimacy together. She is familiar with His touch. Sometimes she feels as if she is clay being molded and formed by His hands.

He embraces her with a husband's uninhibited love. People say love is blind, and His love seems to prove the thought to be true. He always thinks she is a beautiful creation.

The intertwining of their passion has called deep treasures to come forth from her life. Such love and acceptance set her free to share their love with others. Her radiant beauty is visible to all. In the natural, we would describe such attractiveness as the glow of romance. By the Spirit, the glory of God is on display in fulfillment of His divine admiration.

Lost in her Lover, she floats in her Bridegroom's love. No words can describe the place she entered. Even if she tried, others wouldn't understand. Human language is totally inadequate for such explanation.

Jesus completed everything required to have His Bride. He's pleased she yielded to the transformation required to become His partner forever.

God also wants us to enter the fullness of *forever* life with Him, where we too will know His continual, inexpressible satisfaction.

Our Kingdom eternity begins the day we receive Jesus as our Savior. His sacrifice gave us the privilege of enjoying God's love and fellowship every day of our lives.

The Bride entered the inner chambers of her King. Once again we hear the words of joy and pleasure the Divine Lover has for His Bride. These expressions of bedroom intimacy describe the King's passion as He magnifies her perfect maturity. She has been delivered from every hindrance that tried to steal her destiny and true identity. By Love's passion she is free to be vulnerable and abandoned to Him. The couple is veiled in the same purity Adam and Eve enjoyed before the fall.

The words of these verses are for us as well. When we come naked before God, allowing Him to search the deep recesses of our heart, soul, and spirit, we find such nakedness to be far greater than lying bare flesh to flesh.

New liberty welcomes the Bridegroom to lavish His words of love freely on His wife. She no longer pushes Him away, or resists Him because she feels too inadequate. She has learned to *receive* from God.

How beautiful your sandaled feet, O Prince's daughter! The curves of your hips are like jewels, the work of a craftsman's hands. **(7:1)**

Isn't it interesting He first admired the feet of His yielded Bride as He declared her endless perfection? He is pleased her divine feet travel in two realms. She can ascend to the Throne of God to enjoy fellowship with the Trinity, and descend to the hurting world to help others find liberty, too.

The word sandals, is also important in this verse. The Holy Spirit created supernatural footwear for her, which protects and keeps her feet from slipping, as she takes the narrow path leading to life. (Matthew 7:14) Obviously, they're gravity free.

When we receive our divine custom-made shoes from God, it's very likely we'll know it. Before I even knew this verse to be personal and real, I received my shoes.

Near the end of a long dream from the Spirit, I suddenly had new shoes on my feet. Surprised and delighted, I showed them to everyone who passed. No one else in my dream seemed interested in what adorned my feet. The shoes fit perfect, shined beautifully, and didn't get wet when I went out in the rain. I received supernatural shoes to wear to places otherwise impossible to travel. Several years past before I understood what the dream was trying to show me.

The Bridegroom acknowledged to His lover He is pleased she learned to walk in the steps of the Spirit. Her feet go *everywhere* He leads. She no longer fears heights, or hesitates to consider if she is willing to go. She's learned instant obedience in quick response to even a glance of His eyes. She knows, without a doubt Satan, and all things, are under her feet because she shares His Throne.

For shoes, put on the peace that comes from the Good News so that you will be fully prepared. (Ephesians 6:15 NLT)

O Prince's daughter (7:1)

When Jesus says, "O" in regard to His Bride, we know it's big. His awe is as the gasp of someone opening a treasure chest, and finding it full of beautiful, precious stones. Perhaps, He didn't even know the wonder of the perfect Bride He created. The exuberant delight of His ownership, their companionship, and oneness forever, almost made Him speechless.

The Bride has become the daughter of the Prince. *He raises up the poor out of the dust, and lifts the needy out of the dunghill; that He may set him with princes, even with the princes of His people.* (Psalm 113:7-8)

The Bride has received the Holy Spirit's supernatural blood transfusion. Royal blood flows through her veins.

King's daughters are among Your noble ladies. (Psalm 45:9)

The curves of your hips are like jewels (7:1)

Imagine this Lover enjoying the curves of His Brides hips. No one else has the pleasure of this woman's nakedness. Her Husband delights in the artistic workmanship of this Kingdom creation. Even though He has seen her this way many times, He never tires of the beauty of her curves, (grace) describing them as jewels. (glory[5]) She is grace-filled perfection.

The work of a craftsman's hands (7:1)

The hands of the Master Creator had a vision for a masterpiece fit for the King. God found her usable material for His work of genius. And she is us! We are perfectly built as a dwelling place for the Holy Spirit. (I Peter 2:5)

Scripture: *He has glorified the places her feet have gone.* (Isaiah 60:13)

Beautiful upon the mountains, are the feet of those that bring good new. (Isaiah 52:7)

I am confident of this very thing, that He who began a good work in you will be faithful to complete it ... (Philippians 1:6)

Thank you for making me so wonderfully complex! Your workmanship is marvelous, how well I know it. (Psalm 139:14 NLT)

He has made everything beautiful in His time ... (Ecclesiastes 3:11)

Prayer: Lord, search the recesses of my heart, soul, and spirit. Set me free from feeling inadequate, and from things I do that hinder me from receiving Your love. Help me know without a doubt You are saying "O" about me. I want to believe You see me as Your treasured bride. I long to hear Your words of love and praise personally.

My Revelation:

Forever II

The Bridegroom continues describing the pleasure of knowing the Bride is His forever.

Your navel is a rounded goblet that never lacks blended wine. **(7:2)**

Only in the privacy of bedroom intimacy is a man free to express his pleasure with his wife's navel. The Holy Spirit wants us to understand just how intimate the relationship has become between the Bridegroom's Spirit and His Bride's spirit.

There's abundance in her center (navel), her soul and spirit, which is filled with pleasing virtues (blended wine).

Your belly is like a heap of wheat encircled by lilies. **(7:2)**

The inner-man (belly) is filled with the Word, which is the Bread of Life. She has become the breadbasket for the world surrounded by purity (lilies). She nourishes all who are hungry from her huge (heap) source of provision (wheat). She is Jesus's storehouse.

***Your breasts are like two fawns, twins of a gazelle.* (7:3)**

Again, her mature breasts represent faith and love. As love increased, faith was perfected because *faith works by love.* (Galatians 5:6) With full maturity in faith and love, others can see *love never fails.* (I Corinthians 13:8)

She knows the truth. Nothing is impossible with God. Her prayers are answered quickly (gazelle). He said, *Ask of Me and I will give you the nations as an inheritance,* (Psalm 2:8) *ask anything in My name and I will do it.* (John14:13) She has asked, and watched as the amazing answers came.

***Your neck is like an ivory tower.* (7:4)**

The Bride is a stately safe tower. Her royal neck turns watching over what concerns the Lord. Purity and humility qualify her to make requests of His Majesty. She comes to Him regarding situations important enough to change the course of history. Moses is an example of having such a privilege when He asked God not to destroy the people. (Deuteronomy 9:26) Esther also saved her nation by having the King's favor. (Esther)

A tower has been completed in the middle of her spirit-house, where once an unfinished staircase stood. At the top of her spiritual tower her neck turns providing safety, just as a light in a lighthouse. She is a prayer warrior standing in the gap between man and God.

Your eyes are the pools of Heshbon by the gate of Bath Rabbim.

Her eyes are a reservoir (pool) of wisdom (Heshbon) reflecting the beauty of eternity in her soul. She makes way (gate) for *Bath-Rabbim*, which prophetically means the daughter of multitudes, or promise of many.[1] Her eyes reflect the vision of a harvest of millions of people coming into God's Kingdom. No wonder the Word commands us to guard our eye gates. (Psalm 101:3) Eyes protected by purity allow a true vision of God's plans.

Scripture: ... *He ascended on high places, and led captive a host of captives, and he gave gifts to men.* (Ephesians 4:8)

For the eye is the lamp of the body. If your eyes are good your whole body will be full of light. (Matthew 6:22)

Prayer: Lord, Thank You these words of affection also describe who You see me to be. Help me grasp the reality of such intimacy with You. I desire to know the experience of Your hands molding me as clay. I ask for my supernatural shoes so I can go to the high places with Your Spirit. What an unusual prayer. Make my life pleasing to You, Lord.

My Revelation:

Discernment

Your nose is like the tower of Lebanon which faces Damascus. **(7:4)**

The Bridegroom continues to describe the majesty of His forever Bride. He started by enjoying the beauty of her feet, and now has reached her face. In this verse, He wants us to know because of purity (Lebanon) she has become discerning (nose). She's His overseer (tower) keeping watch over the nations from the high places (Damascus).[1]

This is the first time her nose is mentioned in Song of Solomon. Only the mature have learned to smell by the Spirit. Once human logic is overcome, and spiritual wisdom gained, we can see, hear, and feel the reality of the supernatural realm.

Discernment, which smell represents, takes time. To discern is to obtain knowledge or awareness of something not yet known. It requires shutting away with the Lord so His scent can permeate us until we represent the fragrance of His character.

We become the fragrance of Christ ...
(II Corinthians 2:15)

When we have this virtue we can quickly detect anything not of Him. For instance, we hear something that sounds like the truth, but it just doesn't smell quite right. That's discernment, or we could call it spiritual intuition.

Nose, as a tower, is like the nose of a watchdog. A hunting dog's sense of smell is hundreds of times keener than a human. They can even distinguish between odors. I'm fascinated as I watch my dog sniff the air or the ground with great curiosity. It always makes me wonder what passed by earlier to cause such interest.

God gives us this virtue for His Kingdom purposes, as well as for our safety. When we hear the alarm of heaven alerting us to be on guard, we learn to stop in our tracks, listen, and follow the Spirit.

One day I was explaining to God why I didn't have time to serve Him more fully. I had lots of excuses because my life was very busy.

His response was, "No, you keep yourself busy doing other things because you're afraid to do what I've asked of you."

I stopped. Sat quietly. Thought.

I'd never considered all the activity as my way of avoiding what I was really meant to do. I repented and asked friends to pray with me about the fear. As they laid hands on me I was delivered from a Spirit of Fear that held me captive as a powerful stronghold most of my life.

Once free, I stepped into a new liberated life. Relishing newfound freedom, I enjoyed doing things I'd never tried before. However, since I wasn't bound by the fear of danger anymore, I recognized fear had given me a false security by reminding me not to take chances. Now, I needed the Holy Spirit to guide me even more or I might do something foolish and hurt myself. Fear that once ruled needed to be replaced with discernment.

Listening ears would be required to hear the Spirit's voice because nothing else was holding me back. My new freedom came with an emphasized on the importance of staying in the steps of the Spirit.

One night, while learning this lesson, I had to walk alone to my car through a dark alley in a big city. It looked very scary. I stopped, checked to make sure the Holy Spirit was with me, felt His assurance there was no danger, and then I quickly and cautiously walked the few blocks. In my car I smiled at how calm I felt, and gave thanks for the hosts of heaven all around me.

When my husband and I have a big decision to make we know we need discernment. We must hear from the Lord. Doors may appear to be open, but we wait for His direction. People pressure us to agree with their plans, but we wait. While in that process, things fall into place smoothing out all the wrinkles to bring the best success. The insight of this virtue has taught us God has perfect timing. When He finally says, "Move," we're ready, and continue to be amazed by the way He works.

A nose of discernment is on guard, as in a tower, watching, ready to pray. What a privilege to be an intercessor who hears the alarm of heaven when the Holy Spirit asks to be allowed to pray through us. In the process we can learn so much. It is sort of like reading the newspaper before it's printed. The Holy Spirit wants us praying for situations around the world before the news breaks. This requires what the nose represents. Discernment.

Scripture: *Solid food is for the mature, for those who because of practice have their senses trained to discern good and evil.* (Hebrews 5:14)

God didn't give us a spirit of fear but of power and love and discipline. (II Timothy 1:7)

... They have noses, but they cannot smell ... (Psalm 115:6)

Prayer: Lord, today I ask for maturity and discernment. Deliver me from fear. Help me discern Your presence. Teach me to wait, and not let other's pressure steal my peace so I can find Your plan. Lord, it's Your will for me to live without fear, guided by discernment. By faith, I Thank You for a nose that knows.

My Revelation:

Forever III

Your head crowns you like Mount Carmel. Your hair is like royal tapestry (or purple); the King is held captive by your tresses. (7:5)

The Queen's royal crown represents mature authority (head). *Mount* is the Kingdom. *Carmel* means fruitful garden.

In the beginning the maiden couldn't be permitted the authority spoken of here. She would have put herself and others in danger. In immaturity, she would have prayed for what seemed right in her own eyes, instead of finding God's will. Only when fully mature and obedient is her hair described as royalty (purple).

Just as a king put Joseph in charge of his entire kingdom, (Genesis 41) King Jesus has found His Bride trustworthy. He has given her the keys to His Kingdom.

The King is held captive by your tresses. Their spirits have intertwined until they have become as strong rope, or a braid. Because she is yielded, she's received His supernatural strength until she holds Him as tightly as He holds her. Of course, in reality, we know it's only because He is a willing captive.

***How beautiful you are and how pleasing, Oh love, with your delights!* (7:6)**

Remember, this verse is yours personally. Truth declares, "You are beautiful." Even if no one else ever told you this, the King of Truth says you're splendid.

But even more than attractive, the Bride is pleasing. The couple has found pleasure just as we see in two earthly lovers. Not the ones in first-love infatuation, but more like lovers who've been together for years. They've found the treasure unselfishness brings. The husband is past wishing she'd change into something he'd like to imagine her to be. After many years, she's still his lovely bride. He's learned to delight in, and enjoy her quirky little personality traits.

Likewise, as unconditional love grew in the wife, she too is accepting, and finds pleasure in having him in her life. Trust has been established. Patience and kindness have become habit. Unity evolved as they faced life's devastations, joys and victories together. She feels blessed to be his, and can clearly pick his laughter out in a crowded room of noisy people. At parties they seem to gravitate through the crowd to be near each other. Brushing hands as they pass still gives each warm fuzzies. Pausing in their busy day to say, "I love you," puts new bounce in their step. The pleasure of belonging to each other is fulfilling, and pleasing.

The Bride pleases her Bridegroom.

O Love, with your delights (7:6)

Once again, we hear the inexpressible "O" from God. The same God who spoke the words, *let there be,* (Genesis 1:3) says, "O Love." He seems overcome, almost speechless, as if coming to the end of Himself, as He declares, "My Completeness."

With your delights. (7:6) It takes a lover to see our delights. We don't know the musical notes in our voice when we speak. Or the ability we have to melt a heart with our smile, or the hope we put in a soul by just a glance. We've never understood the power of a kiss on a scratched knee, or the courage and strength that comes from a word in due season. We've only glimpsed at what it does for someone when we believe in them. We may miss the light of hope they find in our eyes, or the peace our touch brings.

But the Bridegroom knows, and He is most pleased!

Scripture: *We all, with unveiled face beholding as in a mirror the glory of the Lord, are being transformed*

into the same image from glory to glory, just as from the Lord, the Spirit.
(II Corinthians 3:18)

The King is enthralled by your beauty ...
(Psalm 45:11).

... As a bridegroom rejoices over his bride so will your God rejoice over you. (Isaiah 62:5)

You are a chosen race, a royal priesthood, a holy nation, a people for God's own possession, that you may proclaim the excellencies of Him who has called you out of darkness into His marvelous light. (I Peter 2:9)

... You have brought me into Your presence forever. (Psalm 41:12 NLT)

Prayer: Lord, Thank You, for the truth that You are delighted with me. This is too wonderful to comprehend. I do want to please You with the pure character You are developing in me. I pray for holy guidance as I learn to live in Your authority. May the delights You see in me bring You great joy. I love seeing Your truth. You think I'm beautiful. I must remember You do not lie.

Palm Tree

Your stature is like that of the palm, Your breasts are like clusters of fruit (or grapes) **(7:7)**

The palm represents strength and majesty. The Bride is a pure reflection of her King's patience, consistency, and long-suffering. She stood strong through trials and test of hurricane force as everything around her was flattened.

She has the stature of the fullness of Christ. (Ephesians 4:13)

As faith and love were established in hope, all other virtues (clusters) were free to grow to full maturity. These divine character qualities are as Canaan grapes (heavenly) that have been pruned and tended to become fruitful.

I said, "I will climb the palm tree; I will take hold of its fruit." May your breasts be like the clusters of the vine **(7:8)**

Our Bridegroom declared, "I told you so. *I said* you are perfect in love, faith, and all virtues."

From the beginning of time, He saw a strong majestic Bride bearing fruit for the Kingdom of God. She didn't believe it was possible, but it happened. He told her so.

The Lord is overjoyed with the way she stretches for heaven. She's not a fragile little maiden anymore. Her established strength is irresistible. He feels like a boy wanting to climb a magnificent tree, but there aren't any branches. He'd have to hug the tree with arms and legs and shimmy up it. He takes hold. And don't you know, when He touches her fruit, it will be multiplied just as the bread and fish in Matthew14:17. He grasped her fruit in His hands, blesses it, and divine abundance feeds millions. He draws close, encompassing her completely. There are no hindrances to keep Him away. Suddenly, He breaks through. Heaven comes down and kisses earth.

Revival fills the land.

Scripture: *The righteous man will flourish like the palm tree ...* (Psalm 92:12)

But indeed, as I live, all the earth will be filled with the glory of the Lord. (Numbers 14:21)

Prayer: Come, Lord Jesus. Come Lord Jesus. Encompass us with Your presence. Make our fruit multiply to feed the world. Come and fill the earth with Your revival glory.

Revival

the fragrance of your breath like apples. (7:8)

Apple prophetically means Jesus, the Word. The Bridegroom has pushed past heaven to get to His Bride. While together, He noticed her breath to be the same fragrance as the Kingdom.

We have been told we speak either death or life. (Proverbs 18:21) The pure Bride's words bring an impartation of life into every situation. She says to the nations, "Receive the Holy Spirit," and they bow low accepting life with King Jesus. She demands the sick and the dead to "Rise and be healed in the name of Jesus." They obey. Freely she lives in two realms, with the King as He moves about on earth, and in the Kingdom of Heaven where she sits with Him on His Throne in the Spirit.

Thus says the Lord of hosts, If you will walk in My ways, and if you will perform My service, then you will also govern My house and also have charge of My courts ... (Zechariah 3:7)

Earlier, the maiden was overcome by the Bridegroom's love. Feeling weak, she asked Him to *feed her an apple,* (2:5) or give her strength to receive more of Him. She also said to Him, *You are my Apple Tree,* (2:3) her covering and protection. She has remained "in Him" and fed on Him until His fragrance permeates from within her.

and your mouth like the best wine. It goes down smoothly for my Beloved, flowing gently through the lips of those who fall asleep. **(7:9)**

The best wine develops as it matures. Her life proves it is possible to have an undefiled tongue. True, no man can tame the tongue, (James 3:8) but the Holy Spirit makes it possible. Over time He gently and firmly showed her good and acceptable language. She keeps a tight rein on her words knowing *when words are many, sin is not absent, and in wisdom she holds her tongue.* (Proverbs 10:19) No evil or careless speech crosses her guarded lips. His life within gave her such authority her words became as fire to be easily received (goes down smoothly).

Once words are spoken; we can never get them back. Every good or evil thing we say is suspended in eternity and continues to influence lives.

Proverbs 18:21 reads *death and life are in the power of the tongue.* Grasping the revelation of the power of words, I asked the Holy Spirit to give me sensitivity to what I spoke, and to help fine-tune my language and voice tones. I didn't want to be responsible for speaking death.

Our privilege is to speak pure life-giving words (wine), and watch as good things flow from heaven. We declare Jesus to the nations in our prayers, and countries bow to His Kingship. Sharing hope can resurrect the walking dead (those who fall asleep).

Sometimes, believers are aware there is a standard of righteousness God wants to establish, but they often grumble and complain about the many things that don't measure up to His plan. We must realize the enemy thrives on our negative words, and he is empowered by them. Because we are people filled with Kingdom authority, our words must always be life-giving seeds of truth that build faith. Words have the power to move heaven to earth. They can annihilate Satan's strongholds. It takes discipline to speak what is good and true so the Kingdom of God will manifest on earth.

Scripture: *The speech of the wise shall continually flow with the pure, clear water of life.* (Proverbs 18:4)

Men shall speak of the power of Your awesome acts; and I will tell of Your greatness, and shall shout joyfully of Your righteousness. (Psalm 145:7)

... the opening of my lips will produce right things.
(Proverbs 8:6)

Prayer: Lord, it's interesting a chapter titled *Revival*
refers to spoken words. We need the reality of using
words of life and faith to see Your Kingdom come.
Give me wisdom and boldness to speak the truth so a
continual flow of heaven's glory can become reality
on earth. I ask my words and voice tones be fine-
tuned by Your grace and love. Empower me, as I
speak to others so a hunger for You will be created in
them.

My Revelation:

I Am Desired by God

The Queen's spiritual house is complete. The finished staircase up the middle has free access. The Holy Spirit finally gave her permission to ascend the steep stairs after what seemed a very long time. In wonder and surprise she climbed, then entered the private quarters of the King. She had asked, sought, and knocked as Jesus said to do. (Matthew 7:7)

The King welcomed her into His chambers. In holy fear and trembling she wondered what would happen as she became naked before her Spirit King. He is mighty and powerful, so she felt vulnerable as her garment dropped to the floor. Admiringly, He walked over and ever so gently covered her with His purple robe of righteousness. By His adoring love she felt His warmth, safety, and protection. This is where we continually find the Lovers.

I am my Beloveds, and His desire is for me. (7:10)

I am! The Bride finally knows who she is. There's no greater peace on earth than the assurance of knowing who you are. The words, *I am* in this verse are like a sledgehammer hitting a stake in the ground. There is no more being tossed to and fro.

Questions, doubts, and fear have finished. She's entered into God and she's not coming out.

The word *desire* reveals even more progress in their supernatural relationship. Three times in this story God said *do no arouse or awaken love until it so desires.* (2:7, 3:5, and 8:4)

God pursues and calls us. As we willingly follow Him by allowing our spirit to mature, He gives times of rest. In those times, love and longing grow in all the empty places made ready for Him.

In verse 2:16 we read, *"My Lover is mine and I am His."* She had gotten what her heart yearned for in knowing her Beloved. Notice though, she still considers herself first in the relationship.

By verse 6:3 she told us, *"I am my Lover's and my Lover is mine."* At that point Jesus was first in their relationship. There was no desire in her to be in charge any longer. She understood her life is to be all about Him, not her.

Verse 7:10 declared, *"I belong to my Lover and His desire is for me."* Finally, she knows belonging to God, and being desired by Him, is ultimate fulfillment.

This is true for us too. *We are desired by God.* To know we belong to God and are desired by Him is the fulfillment of the search of every soul. It is time we believe this truth and own it.

Scripture: ... *The King will desire your beauty; because He is your Lord, bow down to Him.* (Psalm 45:11)

... *I have chosen you, declares the Lord of hosts.* (Haggai 2:23)

Prayer: How amazing Lord, I'm desired by You, and belong to You. You chose me. I'm so grateful. I claim this truth as my own today, and ask You to help me believe these words continually. I choose to be an example of a life transformed by love. Thank You, for loving me.

My Revelation:

Let's Go

Come, my Beloved, let us go out into the country, and let us lodge in the villages. **(7:11)**

Coming from a shut away time complete with the contentment of desires fulfilled, the Bride has supernatural energy, purpose, and stability. Now, she takes the initiative to do what she knows will please her Lord. The Beloved said, *Go into all the world and preach the gospel.* (Mark 16:15) *She* said, "Let's go." He no longer needs to call her to come away. She is ready and wants to be a co-laborer with Him.

The Bride is interested in everything happening on earth. She doesn't have a so-called ministry of her own. Wherever she goes and whatever He shows her to do, she does without pause. She has acquired divine flexibility, a rare quality among God's saints, and feels at home in any nation, or tribe of people on earth, as well as in the Throne room of God.

She wants to share His love with everyone. Each opportunity brings joy and fulfillment, whether it's mentoring one soul to know Jesus, or declaring His Word to congregations of thousands. Spending time singing to a sweet baby is as thrilling as raising the dead.

Let us go early to the vineyards, to see if the vines have budded, if their blossoms have opened, and if the pomegranates are in bloom— there I will give you my love. **(7:12)**

The Bride said, "Let's go now (early). We want to watch Your new works (budding vines) and the mature established works (opening blossoms[1]) come together."

What an exciting time these words describe. The old knowledge stored in the hearts of the mature body of Christ blends with the Spirit's fresh revelation. The pure thought life (pomegranates) of His people have finally overpowered grumbling and hopelessness. A standard of righteousness reigns over the nations as the focus becomes Jesus's promises and not what the enemy does. They understand the power of words and thoughts affect the world, so they choose to live in the truth of Philippians 4:8 (NLT). *...Fix your thoughts on what is true, and honorable, and right, and pure, and lovely, and admirable. Think about things that are excellent and worthy of praise.*

She said, "I'm going to pour Your love on others in the same way I love You because You live in them.

As I serve them I will adore the reality of Your presence in their lives."

Loving people with Jesus's love releases them to welcome Him, creating more hearts who freely follow God.

The new work is wonderful. In the past serving was exhausting. Her labor as His servant required so much time and energy she was distracted from focusing on Him and often lost the joy of their fellowship.

By perfection, the Lord's work, and the Lord have become one. Everything she does gives expression of her passion for Him. He continually encompasses her as they do His work together. She is *a partaker of the divine nature having escaped the corruption of this world.* (II Peter 1:4)

When I studied these verses and received the revelation I've shared I heard the Holy Spirit say, *there will come a day when you will be sent out to live this verse. You will recognize it.*

I couldn't imagine how that would happen. In the meantime I spent several years, in what felt like, being shut away. Perhaps, I was living the verses which says *do not awaken until she's ready.* I waited as God put everything together for us to go out.

Our hearts filled as the door of opportunity opened for us to travel our country. We were privileged to attend some of the nation's thriving churches and met so many great people. The precious folks of rural America made us smile as we read signs in the front of their homes giving glory to God.

Feeling newly awakened and inspired, we found delight in every place we traveled. The variety of cultures with their music, food, and sports were fun to learn about. There was so many different ways they earn their income, too.

There's a great shift taking place in our country. People are uprooting to do something different. Some are selling their houses to be ready to go, they don't know where. The army of God is rising. The harvest has begun.

Reports may come out as to how bad things are, but I declare God is blessing nations, and He isn't finish yet. His glory has just begun to rest on us. The days ahead ... well, just watch. Better yet, get involved.

Song of Solomon holds keys to the prophetic revelation of today's Kingdom harvest. Jesus is ready to sow and reap a revival harvest in a way the world has never seen. He has matured a strong Bride, who is living in Jesus's power and love, ready to hear His divine directions.

These are the days Amos 9:13 prophesied. *Behold, days are coming, declares the Lord, when the reaper will overtake the plowman and the planter by the one treading grapes.*

These prophetic words describe a revival so colossal it looks like farmers planting seed, and going through fields harvesting with combines at the same time. They're plowing ground, planting vines, and making wine (treading the grapes) in one day.

Amos's words are describing "now." God has set everything up. He has opened the windows of heaven, prepared the hearts of men as fertile soil who are ready to follow Jesus. They're maturing so fast we're going to hear Christian babies declare the Truth in purity and holiness almost instantly.

Scripture: *The whole earth will acknowledge the Lord and return to Him. All the families of the nation will bow down before Him.*
(Psalm 22:27 NLT)

God elevated Jesus to the place of highest honor and gave Him the name above all other names, that at the name of Jesus every knee should bow, in heaven and on earth and under the earth, and every tongue confess that Jesus Christ is Lord, to the glory of God the Father. (Philippians 2:9-11 NLT)

Prayer: I say "Yes Lord." Complete Your good work. Bring in the mighty harvest. Get us to the place we can be the most effective in declaring Your Kingdom love. What amazing exciting days You have planned for us. Fill Your bride with the energy to accomplish Your will for this hour. Release divine health so none will be held back from the destiny You've prepared for them.

My Revelation:

Beyond Comprehension

The mandrakes send out their fragrance, and over the door are all manner of choice fruits, both new and old, which are laid up for you, Oh my Beloved. (7:13)

Mandrakes are a plant said to cause passion, once considered an aphrodisiac for fertility. (Genesis 30:14). They represent the union between man and wife.

This plant is being used to describe the power that brings God's plans into a final crescendo, just as a beautiful piece of music.

The Bride prophetically stated what God was doing. His revival glory has covered the whole earth, birthing passion for Him in the hearts of mankind. Many babies are born into the Kingdom. The heavenly realm (over) is open (door) revealing cherished prizes.

God hasn't forgotten any of the things the Bride gave Him in the past. All the dreams and hopes for a better day have been redeemed and restored (laid up). He still holds every prayer she prayed. Answers await.

We've given up, or forgotten, many childhood dreams. Things such as what we wanted to do when we grew up. But God hasn't forgotten. When we faithfully surrender everything to Him, both good and bad, He saves them as His treasures. Through time the touch of heaven added value to each of those dreams.

Other things, the fleshly desires of selfishness and pride are marinated in holiness and transformed into pure surprises. God wastes nothing.

She sees, but can't comprehend all that's being shown of her new adventures. There are undisclosed places to go. Unknown plans, yet to be revealed. The Kingdom is forever an odyssey.

For I am accomplishing a work in your days. A work which you will never believe, though someone should describe it to you. (Acts 13:41)

If only You were to me like a brother, who was nursed at my Mother's breasts! Then, if I found you outside, I would kiss You and no one would despise me. I would lead You and bring You to my Mother's house—she who has taught me. I would give you spiced wine to drink, the nectar of my pomegranates. His left arm is under my head and His right arm embraces me. (8:1-3)

The Bride knows what it is to live in the spiritual Kingdom of God. She finally grasped the fact that her Lord is *true reality*. He no longer goes mountain climbing without her. They're in communion twenty-four hours, seven days a week. She hears His words of love, adoration, and devotion continually. What a rapturous expression of love's relationship.

They've been reaping the harvest together. She's seen and experienced supernatural wonders beyond belief. The greatness of her Lover's signs, wonders, power, and love are mind-boggling.

The last tug of earth pulls at her as she reflects on the past. In the same way we remember a place we enjoyed living with people we loved, she has memories of the life she once knew. There's no regrets, just memories. Her prophetic words mingle with thoughts of her earthly family intertwined with new Kingdom knowledge, and her heavenly experiences. We'll call this Brain Overload.

Instantly, Jesus is at her side announcing she'll be resting a while. Knowing how hard she is trying to understand all she has encountered with her natural mind, He wraps her in His arms.

Daughters of Jerusalem, I charge you: Do not arouse or awaken My love until she desires. (8:4)

The Bride is perfect in purity, and *the pure in heart sees everything pure.* (Titus 1:15)

Transformation opened her eyes to see as Jesus sees. Holiness allowed clear vision of Jesus and His Kingdom.

However, with spirit-eyes open, she also understands His Words *all have sinned and fallen short of the glory of God.* (Romans 3:23)

Before, she had little comprehension of the power or disgust of the demonic realm. However, her pilgrimage brought battles which felt like being in a horror movie. Although she's always victorious because of Jesus's name and His blood sacrifice, the supernatural kingdoms have stretched her in unfathomable ways.

She remembers the many strange creatures she encountered, the sensational experiences, and the glorious, spectacular beauty of God's kingdom. And the power, oh, the power is beyond expression. Incomprehensible. Then there's the love. How does one find words? His love keeps multiplying, escalating, even proliferating. Such love could never be contained.

The Bridegroom holds His Bride, allowing her to rest and prepare for her new call. She has seen humanities devastation, and her heart is full of love for her world. She is a worthy Queen for the King.

In this rest, He will give her the blueprint for reaping the harvest of the hour, an important key for us to grasp moving into today's worldwide revival. As we seek His direction for ourselves, we'll marvel at our part in seeing millions come into the Kingdom of God. Everything will supernaturally come together with big impact as the united Bride moves in God's power, plans, and purpose.

Scripture: *She is a chosen people, a royal priesthood, a holy nation, a people for God's own possession that she can proclaim the excellences of Him who called her out of darkness into His marvelous light.* (I Peter 2:9).

The latter glory of this house will be greater than the former, says the Lord of hosts ... (Haggai 2:9)

Prayer: Thank You, for the restoration and redemption of all things Lord. I'm filled with excitement and expectation for our future adventures. I need a brave spirit to enjoy the unusual challenges You have for me. Help me find the powerful glory of being in Your Spirit so I can receive your plans for my life, and fight the good fight of faith.

My Revelation:

The Gift of Weakness

Who is this coming up from the wilderness leaning on her Lover? (8:5)

This verse asks the question, "Who's coming from a place we've never been?" The word wilderness describes *unknown places,* or *the Spirit realm.*

The Bride's spirit has ownership of her soul and flesh. She's been with the Holy Spirit in the radiant beauty of the Kingdom's holiness, and she is holy. With her spirit-eyes open she enjoys the blinding glory of God.

She is part of humanity, but lives in Jesus as He holds her in His arms. Her own strength is gone. She can't even walk (leaning) on her own because gravity no longer holds her captive. Jesus is her everything, including strength, stability, and foundation.

The Holy Spirit has ownership of every cell of her surrendered soul. She's cocooned in Holiness, and experiencing divine metamorphosis. For her, the wilderness is right in the middle of the Glory Realm.

Imagine what she experienced encompassed by Jesus in the stunning realms of heaven. She knows imposing splendor beyond understanding, and inexpressible beauty. Colors, shapes, and sounds never seen or heard on earth. With the revelation of such ecstasy her skin shines brilliantly from the Kingdom's pure light. She reflects God's glory just as Moses did when he was shut away with Him. (Exodus 34:29)

In this rest the Holy Spirit perfected the *Gift of Weakness* in her. As sure as Jacob was touched by Heaven to make him weak, (Genesis 32:25) she has received divine weakness. In the same way Paul served God with a thorn in the flesh to keep Him humble, (II Corinthians 12:7) the Bride has no strength of her own. How strange His perfect strategy was to make her weak.

Before, His strength made her beautiful, powerful, and radiant. Now, completely weak, others don't see her beauty anymore. All they see is *someone* leaning on her Lover.

Humanity now sees Jesus instead of the Bride. She has melted into nothingness as He became everything. By holy fusion, Jesus is clothed by her flesh becoming visible to man.

As the Bride leans on His arm, she finds sweetness in her helplessness. She glories in her weakness, and even rejoices in hard thing, knowing *His power is made perfect in her weakness.* (II Corinthians 12:9)

Under the Apple Tree I roused you; there your Mother conceived you, there she was who in labor gave you birth. (8:5)

Through finding weakness and nothingness the Bride is completely transformed. The Bridegroom explains the Trinity's work of salvation. God the Father longed for His people. The Holy Spirit (mother) planted seeds of faith in her soul (conceived you). Jesus (apple tree) made the way for her to be born again. The divine work (labor) is complete.

Scripture: *Put on the new self, created to be like God in true righteousness and holiness.* (Ephesians 4:24)

… glory … is sown in weakness, it is raised in power. (I Corinthians 15:43)

… God has chosen the weak things of the world to shame the things which are strong … that no man should boast before God. (I Corinthians 1:27)

Prayer: Lord, Your Kingdom is a puzzle. You give us a gift of weakness to bring power. It doesn't sound like a very desirable gift. I must remember Your ways aren't my way. I know I can trust in Your goodness and love even when I don't understand what You're doing. I say, "Yes Lord" to the gift of weakness.

My Revelation:

The King's Seal

Place me like a seal over your heart, like a seal on your arm; (8:6)

Just as a rancher brands his cattle to verify they belong to Him, the Lord marks His people. Some have known the fire-brand of God on their heart as He marked His possession with a seal. This is like a *Stamp of Approval,* only better. God's stamp declares we have given Him ownership of our lives.

Those passionately desperate for God will press into the pain of being branded. I had read about people having this experience. However, my character was to run if pressure got too uncomfortable in life, or in the Spirit. Finally, I realized I would never know all God had for me if I didn't press into His difficult experiences.

Little did I know God had prepared me for even more new challenges. We were worshiping when His presence encompassed us powerfully. Pain began to burn in my heart. I questioned if the heaviness was God or a heart attack. I knew His touch wasn't always pleasant, so I chose to trust I was physically fine, and believe the discomfort was something He was doing. I thought, *I will press into the pain and not back off. I'll stay in this holy spot and see what God wants to do.*

I allowed God's burning to pierce deeply. It hurt as if fire was blazing a hole into my chest, but I didn't run away. All I could do when it subsided was buckle to the floor in weakness. What had happened? Perhaps, I have a brand on my heart now, or maybe I needed a healing. I didn't have a clue. All I know is it was good, because it was God.

It doesn't seem as if God would allow pain, but He isn't always gentle by our definition. Sometimes His touch is so powerful it's frightening and even hurts. Can you imagine the restraint it takes for *All Powerful God* to control His touches of love for us?

I've read some of the great saints had to beg for the Holy Spirit to lift off them, because they couldn't stand anymore of Love's powerful presence. We want to be people who give the Lord complete ownership of ourselves so we are ready to receive our wonderful, frightening God anyway He chooses.

The seal on the arm is the same as the emblems used by the military, police, etc. Their arm badges show they have authority. The Captain of the Host seals His warriors to declare His united army is prepared in power and purpose for battles to liberate nations. The enemy must bow to the seal's authority as we move forward.

Scripture: ... *When you believed, you were marked in Him with a seal, the promised Holy Spirit.* (Ephesians 1:13)

He sealed us and gave us the Spirit in our hearts as a pledge. (II Corinthians 1:22)

...We have the seal of ownership, of family, for the Lord knows those who are His ... (II Timothy 2:19)

So do not grieve the Holy Spirit of God, with whom you were sealed for the day of redemption. (Ephesians 4:30)

Prayer: Lord, I never considered that Your touch would be too overwhelming. Obviously, I don't really know Your ways. So again, I ask You to prepare me for everything You have for me. I want to be fearless before Your revealed glory. I say, "Yes Lord," allowing You to brand me with Your seal. Help me recognize what's happening when You do this, so I don't run from it. I will press into Your fire-love.

My Revelation:

Death's Sting

For love is as strong as death, jealousy is as severe as Sheol. Its flashes are flashes of fire, the very flames of the Lord. (8:6)

The thought of death has been a stranglehold on us throughout human history. However, in knowing Jesus as Savior, death is meant to lose its power. Here's what the scriptures tell us.

We had the sentence of death in us so we wouldn't trust in ourselves, but in God who raises the dead. Who delivered us from the great peril of death, and will deliver us. (II Corinthians 1:9-10)

The last enemy that will be abolished is death. (I Corinthians 15:26)

Jesus has delivered my soul from death so I can walk before God in the light of the living. (Psalm 56:13)

Death where is your victory? O death, where is your sting? The sting of death is sin. (I Corinthians 15:55-56)

289

In the way of righteousness is life, and in its pathway there is no death. (Proverbs 12:28)

I want to know Him, and the power of His resurrection, and the fellowship of His sufferings, being conformed to His death so I can attain resurrection from the dead. (Philippians 3:10)

In unity, we agree with God as He declares over us, *"For I am jealous for you with a godly jealousy; for I betrothed you to one husband, that I might present you as a pure virgin.* (II Corinthians 1:9-10)

The One who is Love longs to see souls complete and fulfilled in their destiny. God's jealous passion fights the spiritual battles required to see His Kingdom established in the hearts of those He desires. His unyielding love *never gives up.*

Our God is a consuming fire. (Hebrews 12:29)

The intensity of God's passionate love bursts forth as He calls us to join Him on His Throne where holy fire is all around. We'll need to live in a fire protective suit, which is Jesus's holiness, as He draws close.

The first experience I had with the Holy Spirit's fire was in a conference during worship. My feet started hurting, and then they felt as if they were burning. I wondered what was wrong. I'd worn my most comfortable shoes.

Everyone in the building got louder as they worshiped. God was moving among us. The burning became hotter and terribly painful. There was no way to get out of the crowd to, perhaps, kick off my shoes to get relief, so I suffered. As the Holy Spirit's presence lifted, the pain left. I grumbled, *Lord, that wasn't fun, it hurt.*

I'd been touched by God's fire-love. With new reverence and awe for my God, I knew coming close to Him was dangerous unless I met Him on His terms, which is holiness.

I'm so grateful for God's gentle patience with me. But His fire-love is coming. It can be with great destructive power as *fire goes before Him and burns up His adversaries round about.* (Psalm 97:3) *Each man's work will become evident for the day will show it, because it is to be revealed with fire: and the fire itself will test the quality of each man's work.* (I Corinthians 3:13)

As Love's power burns, sin and death are destroyed. God's power and purity annihilates anything in our path that might keep us from getting to Him. In the Spirit, His fire is similar to a forest fire's roaring blaze that burns until the land looks flattened. *It burns like blazing fire and a mighty flame.* (8:6)

Sin will be destroyed making a clear path open to heaven.

Knowing the King as Love makes true heroes of people. They willingly lay down their lives for others. By *Love* the Bride's life became a victorious competitor for death. Fear of death has been destroyed, and she is overwhelmed by her love for others.

Scriptures: *From on high He sent fire into my bones* ... (Lamentations 1:13)

He makes ... flames of fire His ministers. (Psalm 104:4)

Love never fails ... (I Corinthians 13:8)

Prayer: Lord, I lay my fear of death at Your feet. I ask You to replace any hold death still has over me with Your love. Help me welcome Your jealousy and fire-love. I pray You find nothing left in me to burn.

My Revelation:

Unquenched Love

Many waters cannot quench Love; rivers cannot wash it away. **(8:7)**

Fire-love can't be quenched. This love has substance. It's vibrantly alive. The complete opposite of emotionless, stagnate, cold death.

During the Bride's rest, her foundation was established by the mighty power of God's love. She *knows* the love described in Ephesians 3:17-19.

That Christ will dwell in your hearts through faith, being rooted and established in love, so you will have the power, together with all the saints, to grasp how wide and long and high and deep the love of Christ, and know this love that surpasses knowledge, that you may be filled to all the fullness of God.

Fire-love has made a path for her. She can see the battles being fought for men's hearts as Satan's demons work in their destructive ways. She uses her authority to set captives free. Evil stands back in fear, trembling as Love passes.

If one were to give all the wealth of his house for love, it would be utterly scorned. **(8:7)**

Matthew 13:45-46 tells a story of a man finding *a pearl of great price*. Jesus and His Kingdom of Love *is* the pearl worth selling everything to own. Love brings sanity into impossible situations. Knowing and owning this treasure imparts the delight of living life fully. Sweet friendships are gifts of love.

Love's passion wants to own our emotions, and establish perseverance that never gives up. This life of love creates the rhythm of our dance, the words of a true poet, and the colors and strokes on a great artist's canvas.

Love is the sacrifice of our Savior, and a parent, and the gratefulness of a worshiper. Its power includes undeserved forgiveness to an unfaithful mate. Love is the covering of all Christ's virtues. We can try to express love in every way possible, but in completion the response is always, *God is love.*

(I John 4:8)

Scripture: *Delight yourself in the Lord and He will give you the desires of your heart.* (Psalms 37:4)

Prayer: Unquenchable love. Do I dare request it to be mine? According to this verse it's permanent, and the most valuable thing I'll ever find. So I say, "Yes Lord." More love is my prayer. Help me know the height and depth of the fullness of who You are as Love.

The Great Commission

We have a young sister, and her breasts are not yet grown. What shall we do for our sister on the day she is spoken for? (8:8)

The completed Bride is in the harvest, and she requests clarity on how to disciple the masses. There's so much to teach them before they can go to the high places and join the ranks of the disciplined, powerful, united Kingdom warriors.

She reports, "Lord, the people have received You into their hearts. They are full of gifts and talents, but they have very little faith and love (breast). They're acting like a bunch of little children with new toys, breaking them as they play. They can't see anything past themselves, and make all sorts of mistakes. What are we to do? How do we begin?"

I found the words of this verse to be a great question. How does one who has experienced so much of the fullness of God relate to newborns? The whole process seemed impossible, especially in light of His harvest that is ready to be reaped.

If she is a wall, we will build towers of silver on her. If she is a door, we will enclose her with panels of cedar. (8:9)

The King answered, "If she is righteous and separated (wall) we'll develop her inner-man as God's dwelling place (build towers) with Jesus's atonement and redemption (of silver[5]). We'll begin construction on her spirit house including a spiral staircase leading to the Throne Room."

Just as each child isn't born with an individual manual, those coming into their full salvation have been uniquely created.

This verse is referring to the five-fold ministries of pastor, evangelist, teacher, apostle, and prophet mentioned in Ephesians 4:11. Each member of the Bride will represent one of those areas of ministry, even though they may fulfill their destiny quite differently.

If she is a wall, she has been created to be a protector. Her call is pastor or prophet. A pastor stands guard protecting as a watchman on the wall. A prophet declares the walls to build up for future protection, encouragement and success.[8]

If she is a door (opening, or entrance) we'll enclose her with panels of cedar (grace, power, beauty, royalty[5]). Door represents an evangelist, or teacher. The evangelist opens the door of salvation. The teacher gives revelation through the Word.[8]

The Bride recognized mentoring a sister is the same as training children. She must watch for their bent, character, and strengths. What gives their life joy? Her job is to direct them in the most effective ways to bring them to maturity and the fulfillment of their destiny.

Our process begins as mentors by sharing our own personal testimony of knowing Jesus, and telling of His amazing goodness.

Of course, teaching them how to love will always be *the number one* goal in their maturing process. Every other success stems from Love.

Like a mother, the Bride will pick up the young when they stumble, encourage them when they fail, and continually show what love looks like. She'll always point them to Jesus who is *All in All*.

Scripture: ... *God makes salvation its walls.* (Isaiah 26:1)

Prayer: Lord, it has taken so much time and effort for me to grow up in You. I find it hard to imagine I have anything to give others. Show me how to help my sisters and brothers fulfill their destiny. I do love them, and it hurts me to see them struggle. I ask for the ability to discern the ministry gifts and talents You want called forth in their lives.

My Revelations:

Come Lord Jesus

I am a wall, and my breasts are like towers.
Thus I have become in His eyes like one
bringing contentment. (8:10)

The Bride suddenly has new revelation of His
righteousness, as she realizes she has been made a
wall of salvation. Her breasts are mature in faith
and love. She *is* a tower of protection and strength.
Oh, how wonderful to *know* *we* bring contentment to
God.

Solomon had a vineyard in Baal Hamon; He
entrusted His vineyard to caretakers (8:11)

Baal Hamon isn't a real city. The prophetic name
means *things to come.* Baal Hamon is interpreted
"the Lord of all" or "the Father of a multitude."[7]

Remember the promise God made to Abraham
when He said his descendants would be as the sand
of the sea? (Genesis 22:17) This vineyard is similar
to that promise, because it describes masses of
people. Revelation 7:9 tells us there's a multitude of
the redeemed around the Throne of God.

Prophetically, the words describe God's end-time
harvest of people (vineyard[5]) which are brought to

Him by His saints (caretakers). He trusts us to nurture, cultivate, and help prune a harvest of souls with His divine grace. We weed and feed as we bring the harvest to full maturity by His leading and power.

Each was to bring for its fruit a thousand shekels of silver. (8:11)

Just as in the parable of the talents (Matthew 25:15) there will come a day when God calls for the profits. *One thousand* is complete maturity[2], which is the requirement of all saints.

We carry Jesus's atonement and sacrifice (silver) as His life flows through us. Therefore, everything we say and do to bless others has value.

I was sitting in the large church we attended early one Sunday morning. As the impressive group of choir members entered, the Lord began to speak to me.

"See Sally? She thinks you're great."

Surprised to hear Jesus say those words, I asked Him why. I hardly knew her.

"Because you knelt down and talked to her daughter five years ago."

I barely remembered who her daughter was.

Jesus went on. "See Jan? She thinks you're special because you sent her a card when she was sick. That one admires you for bringing the cookies you made to the meeting."

He continued on about how big the nothing things I'd done were in the Kingdom realm. Some things He mentioned, I couldn't even remember.

A cup of cold water given in His name has eternal value. A gentle touch can calm those in despair. A word in due season has the power to set captives free. That's valuable. Nothing is wasted with God. The King has made us relevant so everything we do is effective.

In ourselves, we've become nothing. But in Him we're all things to all people. (I Corinthians 9:19-23) We come as a touch from heaven, and bring with us a breath of divine air. We may be the light on another's paths to help them find their way. By our little acts of kindness Heaven is enlarged. We're relevant to the Kingdom of God.

But my own vineyard is mine to give; the thousand shekels are for You, O Solomon, and two hundred are for those who tend its fruit. (8:12)

The Bride is pleased her own garden is flourishing. In the beginning, she made excuses for the failure of her unkempt garden. Now she has (or is) a profitable vineyard, and it's hers to give if she wants.

According to the law of righteousness, the keepers were to pay Solomon a thousand pieces of silver. Although she is in a love relationship with Him, she won't give less than the Lord's duty requires.[4]

Filled with gratitude for the Holy Spirit's tender care of her fruit the Bride gave Him a material token as her worship. Through her entire journey of growth, He became her guide, companion, friend, strength, perseverance, grace, and mercy. She will not deny Him His portion.[4]

O You who sit in the gardens, My companions are listening for Your voice. Let Me hear it. **(8:13)**

Now Jesus, the Bridegroom speaks to His Father, and to the Holy Spirit *(You who sit in the gardens).* "Father, only You know the day and the hour I return, but surely the time has come."

Father God looks at the Bride-united knowing their ears are tuned to heaven. They lift their heads listening for His voice. Their spirits are energized with anticipation, and they hope it is finally time for Jesus's return.

Hurry, my Beloved and be like a gazelle or like a young stag on the mountains of spices. **(8:14)**

The Bride cries, "Come quickly (gazelle) in fulfillment of all Your promises (spices).

The harvest is in, man and Spirit are One. The sound of lovers wanting each other calls out. Just as doves coo to one another, love's call echoes as the Bride and her Beloved beckon to each other in love's completeness.

The Bride continues ... *Come Lord Jesus.*

He answers, *Yes, I am coming quickly.*

(Revelation 22:20)

Heaven and earth kiss. *The Kingdom of the world has become the Kingdom of our Lord and of His Christ and He will reign forever and ever.*

(Revelation 11:15)

Scripture: *We confess that we are strangers and aliens on earth. We are seeking a country of our own. We desire a better country that is a heavenly one. Therefore, God is not ashamed to be called our God; for He has prepared a city for us.* (Hebrews 11:13-16)

For you have come to Mount Zion to the city of the living God, the heavenly Kingdom and to myriad of angels, to the general assembly and church of the first-born who is enrolled in heaven, and to God the Judge of all and to the spirits of righteous men made perfect and to Jesus. (Hebrews 12:22)

So we fix our eyes on Jesus, the author and finisher of our faith. (Hebrews 12:2)

Prayer: Thank You, Lord that I am one who brings You contentment. I *will* believe this truth. Thank You, even though I don't often realize it, everything I do by Your leading is relevant. Help me consciously look for ways to bless others today.
Lord, awaken Your Bride to the mighty rapturous glory You have for us. Give us insight on how we are to help prepare all Your bride to be One with You. Oh, please, open the heavens and kiss earth. Let Your Kingdom come today. We love You, Lord, and I agree by saying, "Come, Lord Jesus.

My Revelation:

Conclusion

Today is the day to live in the fullness of the salvation Jesus provided. Wherever we are in our spiritual walk, we are meant to realize there is always more to the adventure of knowing our glorious God. His awesome Kingdom realm is a continual surprise of life and love.

We begin by humbling ourselves and yielding to God's mighty works. The unknown always comes with challenges and struggles, but it's interesting overcoming the trials of the hard, scary places is what makes the great memories. We have the privilege of stepping out of fear and into faith so we can launch into God's supernatural Kingdom adventures.

As guide, the Holy Spirit will lead us to the Banqueting Table, the House of Wine, His Verdant Bed of Life, and the Secret of the Stairs. We'll ride in the Chariot of the Prince, and know all the experiences of the Apple Tree. Salvation will lie in our heart like myrrh. The privilege of embracing suffering for Jesus sake, and the joy of sharing His fellowship in our inner garden will become reality.

We'll learn to recognize the authority He has assigned to us, and experience the secrets of the

Wilderness. He has made the way for us to live in freedom which comes as faith and love matures. Amazing! He wants us to know His embrace as we share His Throne, and experience Jesus's ravished heart of love. Victory will be found as we press into the pain required to receive His seal on our heart, which also brings the Gift of Weakness. By such sacrifices, His power is released within us. Metamorphosis evolves in being shut away to cocoon in Holiness. We'll marvel at God's signs, wonders, and miracles as we bring a harvest of souls into the Kingdom of God, and experience the delight of mentoring the masses who cry, "Come Lord Jesus." (Revelation 22:17)

We've come to the end of the Song, but we're only beginning to know the fulfillment of our destiny as we live *in Christ*, and experience the glory of God's plans for our eternity (time without end).

Scripture: *He that overcomes, I will make a pillar in the temple of My God, and he will not go out from it anymore; and I will write upon him the name of My God, and the name of the city of My God, the new Jerusalem, which comes down out of heaven from My God, and My new name.* (Revelation 3:12)

He who overcomes, I will grant to him to sit down with Me on My Throne, as I also overcame, and sat down with My Father on His Throne. (Revelation 3:21)

May grace and peace be multiplied to you in the knowledge of God, and of Jesus our Lord, seeing that His divine power has granted us everything pertaining to life and godliness, through the true knowledge of Him who called us by His own glory and excellence ... that we might become partakers of the divine nature. (II Peter 1:3)

Prayer: Yes, Lord. That's all I can say. I long for You. I yearn to live Your adventure. Thank You, for opening my spirit-eyes to new thoughts and possibilities in Your Word. I realize I've only begun to know You and Your amazing ways. Help me be aware of the Holy Spirit guiding me into Your Kingdom life every moment. Thank You, for the awesome privilege of knowing Your love.

My Revelation:

Let the people of Mount Zion be glad,
Let the daughters of Judah rejoice,
Because of Your judgments.
Walk about Zion, and go around her;
Count her towers;
Consider her ramparts;
Go through her palaces;
That you may tell it to the next generation.
For such is God,
Our God forever and ever,
He will guide us until death.
Psalm 48:11-14

Let the Adventure Begin!

References

1. Christ and His Bride - Cora Harris MacIlravy
2. Dream Encounter Symbols – Barbie Breathitt
3. The Song of the Bride - Jeanne Guyon

   Madame Guyon: Lived from 1648-1717. She was a French Catholic. Called a mystic for her understanding of the things of the Spirit. She was persecuted, and put in prison for her love and passion for God and for having insight into the things of the Spirit we are just learning. *An Autobiography Madame Guyon* tells her story.

4. The Song of Songs - Watchman Nee
5. Interpreting the Symbols and Types – Kevin J. Conner
6. Practicing the Presence of God – Brother Lawrence
7. God's Ravished Heart – Iverna Tompkins
8. The Secret of the Stairs – Wade E. Taylor
9. Reference unknown

Scripture References: Song of Solomon scriptures are from the New American Standard Bible. Other verses are also from New International Version.

www.ingramcontent.com/pod-product-compliance
Lightning Source LLC
Chambersburg PA
CBHW072002060426
42446CB00042B/1368